The Walnut Cookbook

Juglandeae.

Juglans regia L.

The Walnut Cookbook

by **Jean-Luc Toussaint**

English edition by

Betsy Draine & Michael Hinden

TEN SPEED PRESS
Berkeley, California

Originally published as
La Noix dans tous ses états: 131 Recettes Gourmandes
© 1994 L'Hydre édition

Ten Speed Press
P.O. Box 7123
Berkeley, California 94707

Distributed in Canada by Publishers Group West,
in New Zealand by Tandem Press, in Australia by Simon and Schuster Australia,
in South Africa by Real Books, in Singapore and Malaysia by Berkeley Books,
and in the United Kingdom and Europe by Airlift Books.

Design by Toni Tajima

Original cover illustration by Claude Guyot

Photographs by Jean-Luc Toussaint
Additional photography by Michael Hinden (p. x, bottom),
and Francis Lasfargues (p. 11)

Library of Congress Cataloging-in-Publication Data

Toussaint, Jean-Luc.
    [Noix dans tous ses états. English]
    The walnut cookbook / Jean-Luc Toussaint;
    translated by Betsy Draine and Michael Hinden.
       p. cm.
    Includes index.
    ISBN 0-89815-948-2
    1. Cookery (Walnuts) 2. Cookery, French. I. Title.
TX814.2.W3T6813   1998
641.6'451–dc21   98-5059
                                                                        CIP
First Printing, 1998

Printed in China

1 2 3 4 5 6 7 8 9 10 — 02 01 00 99 98

Table of Contents

Acknowledgments

For their help and encouragement as we prepared the English edition, we are grateful to our food-loving friends, especially those who tasted, tested, and talked walnut cooking with us: Louise Root Robbins and Ken Robbins, Judy and Ben Sidran, Buck and Ann Rogers-Rhyme, Arnaud and Valerie Delmontel, Melissa Reed, Giovanna Miceli Jeffries, Julia Edwards, Barbara Flaherty, Sandy Schuette, and Dr. Lewis Leavitt.

Most of all, we thank Jean-Luc Toussaint for the opportunity to bring his creative, yet traditional walnut recipes to an English-speaking audience.

Betsy Draine
Michael Hinden

Preface to the English Edition

This may be the first cookbook dedicated entirely to walnuts. It was originally published in France by our colleague Jean-Luc Toussaint under the title La Noix dans tous ses états: 131 Recettes Gourmandes. Toussaint is a talented cook, author, and folklorist who specializes in the history and customs of old Périgord, the region in southwestern France since renamed the Department of the Dordogne, after the river that carved its landscape. The region lies 100 miles inland from Bordeaux, roughly between Bergerac to the west and Cahors to the southeast, with the beautiful medieval town of Sarlat at its center. The area is known for its robust cuisine. Périgord is home to the truffle, goose liver pâté, strawberries, and walnuts, which the people of the region have used in their cooking for generations. Some of the recipes included here are variations of traditional dishes; others are Jean-Luc's free inventions, based on creativity and experiment.

Jean-Luc is our closest neighbor in the hilltop village of Castelnaud-la-Chapelle, near Sarlat, where we have spent our summers for the past ten years. The kitchen window of our small stone cottage faces his front door. And through that window, over the summers, have passed, first, cheery greetings as we both prepared our evening meals, then tidbits of particular dishes to sample. Eventually we shared dinners and conversations about food. The result of this exchange is this collaborative effort, a revised and expanded version of La Noix dans tous ses états designed for an American audience. The recipes have been translated, converted to English weights and measures, and sometimes modified in accordance with American cooking techniques and ingredients available in the United States. The introduction ("All About Walnuts") is expanded from the French and contains new information on the health benefits of walnuts.

Before sampling the recipes, American readers are invited to take a tour of the walnut in all of its forms (La Noix dans tous ses états). More than a nutritious snack, the walnut has a fascinating history and has played an important role in the lives of the people of Périgord. Tracing the story of the walnut offers a glimpse into the culture of rural France, especially of the last century.

Even today in farming hamlets and small villages such as Castelnaud, some of the old customs hang on. The village of Castelnaud-la-Chapelle winds up the side of a steep rocky hill with an imposing medieval château rising above it. During the tourist season, hordes of visitors crowd its lanes during midday, but in the evening and early morning hours the village breathes to an older rhythm. The setting sun colors the limestone houses a shade of honey yellow, and when it dips behind the hills, the residents come out to water their gardens and gossip. In the morning, fog often rolls up from the valley below, leaving the stones of the village a moldy gray.

On such a morning, one of our first as home owners in the village, we walked down to the little square by the *mairie* (the town hall) and stumbled, it seemed, into the nineteenth century. An old woman wearing a blue print apron (Madame Bournazel, then in her nineties) sat in front of her house with a basket of walnuts next to her and a thin slab of *lauze* (a flat stone used for roofing tiles in old Périgord houses) on her lap. She was cracking walnuts with an antique wooden mallet. With amazing dexterity, she picked walnuts from her basket and cracked them on the stone, breaking the shells in a single stroke of her mallet, using just the right amount of force to ensure that the kernels were retrieved whole. Her husband, who was nearly 100 and wore blue coveralls and a faded beret, sat next to her and helped with the sorting.

We struck up a conversation with monsieur and learned that the couple's daughter-in-law, who kept a café in the village, used the nuts in confections she sold to the tourists. Her specialty was *gâteaux aux noix,* dry walnut cakes baked without flour and sold in small tins. We later sampled some, and they were delicious. Another specialty was her *confiture de noix,* a breakfast spread made of sugar and walnut paste that is scrumptious on a croissant.

We learned more about walnuts on that morning: how they can be used in an amazing variety of dishes; how during the war, when people had little to eat, whole families depended on the walnut crop for their main source of protein; how ownership of a stand of walnut trees was a source of pride and status in the countryside; how, in the village, walnuts were associated with longevity; how a bag of walnuts hanging from a kitchen ceiling beam meant that there were plenty to go around and that a fistful might be pressed upon a visitor.

The next morning we awoke to find a bag of walnuts on our doorstep, along with string beans and potatoes from the garden of another neighbor. At first light, Madame Roulland, a widow in her eighties, had climbed the steep path to our door to welcome us with a gift. In the summers since, we have enjoyed the bounty of Madame Roulland's garden and the friendship of our neighbors in the village. A net bag of walnuts always hangs in our kitchen to remind us of our welcome, for our romance with the fruit was sealed that first summer. This beginning has led, a decade later, to *The Walnut Cookbook*: a tribute to the walnut, the palate, and the hearty people of Périgord.

Betsy Draine
Michael Hinden

The village of Castelnaud-la-Chapelle at the end of the 19th century.

Castelnaud today, with its restored castle. The homes of the author and translators are visible in the foreground.

All About Walnuts

THE PÉRIGORD PARADOX

A few years ago, wine drinkers were cheered by the news that wine, particularly red wine, when taken in moderation might actually be healthy for the heart. The topic was popularized by Morley Safer in a CBS *60 Minutes* segment in 1991 and then by Lewis Perdue's book *The French Paradox and Beyond: Live Longer with Wine and the Mediterranean Lifestyle.* The "paradox" is that the French suffer nearly 50 percent fewer heart attacks than Americans, despite their high-fat diet, aversion to exercise, and addiction to cigarettes. For Perdue and his medical colleagues, the evidence suggested that red wine might be the cleansing agent that kept Gallic arteries open when, by rights, the French should be dropping in record numbers at the dinner table after their cheese and dessert courses.

Wine alone may not be the entire explanation. According to Dr. R. Curtis Ellison, food and lifestyle also contribute to the health benefits enjoyed by the French. He observes that the French (1) consume moderate, regular amounts of alcohol, mainly wine taken with meals; (2) eat more fruits and vegetables than Americans; (3) dine more leisurely and avoid snacks; (4) consume less red meat; (5) eat more cheese but drink less milk; (6) use more vegetable oils and less lard and butter in their cooking.

But there may be another wrinkle to the French Paradox. Surprisingly, cardiovascular disease is even lower in southwestern France than elsewhere in the country, despite the fact that Périgord's cuisine is the richest in all France: duck, pork, and goose products, including the famous foie gras, consumed whole or in pâtés; omelettes with truffles fried in goose fat; *rillettes* (shredded fowl and fatty pork terrine); *cou farci* (goose neck stuffed with sausages); and the signature dish of the region: *confit de canard*, cooked duck preserved in its own melted fat, kept in jars or tins, then reheated and served with sliced potatoes fried in the remaining fat—followed by a *cabécou* (dried goat cheese) and pastry.

Wine accompanies the meal and sometimes precedes it—poured in a soup bowl and gulped according to a custom known as *faire chabrol*. But the amount of wine consumption in the region does not distinguish it from other provinces. So the search for the "Périgord Paradox" continues. How do *les Périgourdins* maintain their health in spite of their rich cuisine? Tantalizing evidence points to the walnut as another protective agent. In that part of France, no meal is complete without a traditional *salade Périgourdine*, or mixed green salad seasoned with walnut oil and sprinkled with chopped walnuts. In Périgord a salad may be more than the fourth course in a long meal; it may serve as an antidote. Recent medical evidence suggests that walnut consumption can lower cholesterol levels in the bloodstream.

Cholesterol is a waxy substance found in animal products that is also produced naturally by the liver. It is carried through the blood by compounds called lipoproteins. Medical experts explain that there are two types of lipoproteins, LDL, which carries the cholesterol that is produced in the liver to the body's cells, and HDL, which collects cholesterol from the cells and carries it back to the liver for processing. HDL helps cleanse the bloodstream and is associated with a decreased risk of heart attack, while LDL can deposit excess cholesterol in the arterial walls and so raise the risk of heart attack. In nonmedical language, LDL is sometimes referred to as the "bad" cholesterol, whereas HDL has been called the "good" cholesterol. Several studies now have shown that walnuts have a beneficial effect in reducing overall cholesterol levels in the body and especially the LDL level, the "bad" cholesterol.

WALNUTS & WELLNESS

One interesting study entitled "Effects of Walnuts on Serum Lipid Levels and Blood Pressure in Normal Men" was published in the March 1993 *New England Journal of Medicine*. This team previously had observed that frequent consumption of nuts was associated with a reduced risk of heart disease. As a follow-up to this finding, they placed two groups of men on controlled diets for four weeks, one of which ("the walnut diet") called for 20 percent of the group's weekly calories to be derived from walnuts. The doctors found that the walnut eaters, compared to the control group, had reductions of 12.4 percent in total cholesterol, 16.3 percent in LDL ("bad") cholesterol, and only 4.9 percent in HDL ("good") cholesterol. The ratio of "bad" to "good" cholesterol was also lowered by the walnut diet.

Another study published in the May 1994 *American Journal of Clinical Nutrition* produced similar results. Saturated fatty acids in the diet were partially replaced with almonds or walnuts. In this experiment, a daily supplement of nuts providing half the total fat intake was added to a common background diet. Compared with the control diet, the researchers found that there were significant reductions in total and LDL cholesterol levels for the almond- and walnut-eating group. The almond eaters showed a 10 percent drop in their LDL level, while the walnut eaters showed a 9 percent drop.

Still another study published in the July 1995 *Journal of the American Dietetic Association* found that antioxidant-rich foods such as walnuts can limit the extent of heart injury following a heart attack.

Long before these studies were conducted, the people of Périgord used walnut oil for cooking and made the walnut salad an integral part of their main meal, realizing instinctively that it was conducive to good health. Our neighbors in the village certainly give credence to the view that walnuts are *"bonne pour la santé"*—as we have been told so many times. Walnuts certainly are rich in proteins and vitamins (C, E, B_1, B_2, B_5, B_6), but to balance the picture, walnuts also are high in calories: about 500 calories per 100 grams (or 3.5 ounces). Fourteen good-sized fresh walnuts will yield about a fifth of an individual's daily caloric needs, so moderate consumption is in order. Incorporating modest quantities of walnuts in recipes may be an ideal way to enjoy their benefits.

Further studies are required to confirm that walnuts can play a significant role in decreasing the risk of heart disease. Also, a small number of people are allergic to walnuts, and for them ingestion can have serious consequences. For most of us, though, walnuts can be enjoyed without risk. As part of a well-balanced diet, they may even play a role in promoting health.

THE WALNUT IN MYTH & HISTORY

The walnut is one of the world's most venerable foods. In Périgord, from Peyrat to Terrasson, excavations have brought to light petrified shells of nuts that were roasted during the Neolithic period, more than eight thousand years ago.

Around 2,000 B.C. in Mesopotamia, the Chaldeans left inscriptions on clay tablets revealing the existence of walnut groves within the famed Hanging Gardens of Babylon. There is evidence of walnut consumption dating from the same era on carved stelae containing the Code of Hammurabi, in a section devoted to food.

In the Old Testament, King Solomon speaks with delight of visiting his walnut grove: "I went down into the garden of nuts to see the fruit of the valley" (Song of Solomon 6:11).

The walnut appears in Greek mythology in the story of Carya, with whom the god Dionysus fell in love. When she died, Dionysus transformed her into a walnut tree. The goddess Artemis carried the news to Carya's father and commanded that a temple be built in her memory. Its columns, sculpted in wood in the form of young women, were called caryatides, or nymphs of the walnut tree—so the tree furnished the image for a famous Greek architectural form.

The very name of the walnut tree and its nut comes down to us from the Romans. *Juglans regia* (walnut tree) and *nux juglandes* (the walnut) stem from *Jovis Glans* or the Royal Nut of Jove. The word for nut itself derives from the Latin *nux* or *nucleus* (fruit of the shell), with a suggested derivation from *nox* (night) owing to the dark juice of the nut, which was used to dye wool.

The walnut and the oil extracted from it, therefore, have been known since ancient times. Theory has it that the walnut may have disappeared in parts of northern Europe during the glacial period but was then reintroduced by barbarian invaders and by Greco-Roman conquerors. Once the tree was reestablished, the exploitation of its products spread steadily through increasing trade.

THE TREE & ITS WOOD

The walnut tree has thrived since before recorded history. The tree grows easily in most temperate climates if sheltered from strong winds and cold. It prefers plains and gentle hills where the soil is deep and permeable, but it is known to grow on mountains, too, up to an altitude of three thousand feet. In Europe, the tree may grow from sixty to eighty-five feet in height and typically measures three feet in diameter. One legendary specimen was sixteen feet in circumference, according to the *French Farmer's Journal.*

The walnut tree.

The single-seeded nuts of the walnut tree contain no endosperm, so each tree carries male and female flowers, which bloom each year in April and May. The trunk is thick and covered with smooth, whitish bark when young, but as the tree matures the bark coarsens and corrugates. Close to the ground the tree's shape is formed by heavy twisting branches that bifurcate and become more delicate as the tree rises, creating an attractive dome shape. The dense leaves constantly seek the sun and, in time, spread out over a considerable area.

There are two main types of walnut in Europe, the *Juglans regia*, native since antiquity, and the black walnut, imported from North America in the seventeenth century. The continued use of the black walnut is doubtful now due to disease. However, its wood is exceptionally hard and still used for furniture, paneling, and musical instruments. The wood of both varieties is prized for wood carving and sculpture, for it is smooth and heavy, with a fine, narrow grain that can be polished to a high gloss. Often the wood contains gnarls and curls that have remarkable changing hues.

In Périgord, the wood continues to be employed in heavy rustic furniture and used for religious statues that decorate cathedrals and village churches. At outdoor fairs during the summer, tourists can find beautiful handcrafted walnut objects for sale. The wood was, and still is, used for gun stocks. Entire groves were depleted during periods of military conflict; one document from the archives of the Department of Corrèze confirms that "the Revolution necessitated heavy cutting of walnut trees around the villages of Argentat, Tulle, and Collonges for the manufacture of arms." During the last century, many common household items were made of walnut: plates, dishes, spoons, farm objects such as water jugs and animal yokes—even wooden shoes.

SUPERSTITIONS

Despite the walnut tree's beauty and usefulness, it has a mysterious reputation in Europe. In Italy in the seventeenth century, the infamous Tree of Benevento was believed to be the haunt of witches. The bishop of the village uprooted it, but another malevolent tree, it was said, grew in its place. Even the shade from walnut trees gave rise to fears. Pliny wrote that the walnut's shadow dulled the brain and was a nuisance to whatever was planted nearby.

In *The Red and the Black,* Stendhal also complained that the tree's shade ruined all other plantings in the vicinity, and it may be true that the tree's roots give off a toxic substance to clear space for their growth. Popular legend holds that it is unlucky to plant walnut trees too close to a stable, because the animals might fall ill and die. Travelers are warned not to spend the night under a walnut tree for fear of catching cold.

Paradoxically, the walnut tree was also credited with special virtues in rural France. Horses were rested in its shade to keep away horse flies. The leaves of the tree, boiled and concocted into an ointment, were said to relieve farm animals of ticks and fleas. Other lotions made from the leaves served as cures for scrofula and chilblain. In some provinces the tree was believed to be endowed with aphrodisiac powers. Suitors were counseled to slip a leaf from the tree into the left shoe of a young lady during the mid-summer festival of Saint Jean in order to win her heart. In the Poitou, a gigantic specimen known as the Bride's Walnut Tree was said to ensure abundant mother's milk if the bride and groom danced around its trunk on their wedding night.

Today walnut trees grow throughout Périgord, in fields, around houses, and along roads and paths. Charming walnut groves grow along the banks of the Dordogne and Céou Rivers, softening the craggy appearance of the two river valleys, which merge near Castelnaud.

WALNUT PRODUCTION

In Europe, France is the leading producer and exporter of walnuts. In the middle of the nineteenth century, when the silk industry in the southeast was threatened by a disease of the silkworm and the wine industry in the south-west was ravaged by phylloxera, these regions turned to walnut production to save their economies. In the southeast, production is concentrated in the Dauphine. In the southwest, production centers around Périgord and covers the departments of the Dordogne, Lot, Corrèze, Lot and Garonne, and part of the Charante. Here the principal varieties are the Franquette, Grandjean, Corne, and Marbot. The town of Sarlat is the traditional center of walnut commerce. As long ago as 1657, Verdier wrote: "Walnut trees are abundant in Périgord and have given rise to an industry of which Sarlat is the capital."

The walnut harvest in Périgord.

The walnut market in Sarlat.

Today, however, the United States is the largest walnut producer in the world. Production is concentrated in California, especially in the Sacramento Valley, and in Oregon. The U.S. varieties owe their origin to the Spanish conquistadores and friars, who brought plantings north from Chile and Mexico. In the latter part of the nineteenth century, French growers introduced their own grafts in the United States, and today the hearty American varieties carry the history of two continents. Many bear the names of their creators: Hartley, Serr, Ashley. Among the most important varieties are the Payne, Eureka, Pedro, Chico, Chandler, and of course, the black walnut.

In France the annual harvest occurs around September 20, but the date changes somewhat from year to year depending on conditions. Traditionally, the French collect walnuts by beating the branches of the tree with long poles to dislodge the nuts, which are then gathered by hand. Today large-scale production requires mechanized collection. Big shaking machines are used to clear the branches, while suction machines on the ground scoop up the fallen nuts.

In France, the product may be marketed as "fresh walnuts" as long as their moisture content remains above 20 percent. If the moisture content falls below 12 percent, they must be sold as "dry walnuts," though they can have a shelf life of a year if kept in a cool place. In the old days the nuts were placed in simple drying racks exposed to the wind but kept out of the sun. Today industrial hot-air dryers are employed, which improve the quality of preservation. By law, any nuts sold after June 1 following their September collection must be labeled "old harvest" on the container. But some store managers practice an old trick: if the walnuts are soaked overnight in water or warm milk, they regain much of their original flavor and appearance.

IN A NUTSHELL

The nut itself is composed of three elements. First there is the kernel, the edible part of the nut, formed by two ivory-colored lobes or hemispheres covered by a dark brown skin.

The second element is the endocarp of the nut, its shell, which has been used in a surprising number of ways over the centuries. Pliny recommended that the shell be crushed and mixed as a cement to fill dental cavities. Louis XI had his barber shave him with heated walnut shells, instead of a razor, to prevent nicks. Bakers spread a powder made from the shells on the platforms of ovens to prevent bread from sticking to the surface. In the aeronautical industry, the powder made from pulverized walnut shells is used as a polish for certain metals, and in the cosmetics industry it has been used in facial powder. Oil riggers use it as an abrasive for their drills. And due to the powder's ability to resist carbonization at extreme temperatures, NASA has used it for thermal insulation in the nose cones of its rockets.

The third element, the pericard, is the husk. It is green, soft, and fleshy and is used in the preparation of a fine liqueur. A walnut stain is also made from the husk, which in earlier times was used to dye hair; it is still used to tint wood. Boiled with the leaves and brewed into a cure-all, the husk was used in the past as a remedy for anemia, rickets, and as a gargle for sore throats. (If that failed, there was always the liqueur.)

WALNUT OIL

One of the most important walnut products is its oil. The kernels are crushed into a paste, gently heated, then pressed into an extract of virgin oil. (Sometimes the paste is pressed without heating, but heating helps bring out the subtle flavor of the nut.) Two kilograms of nuts (4.4 lbs.) will yield a liter (slightly less than a quart) of oil. The oil is savory, transparent but golden, and delicious right out of the bottle as a light salad dressing or seasoning for steamed vegetables (try it on string beans) or fish. Like olive oil, it is rich in vitamins and low in saturated fatty acids. Yet because of its high caloric content (260 calories per ounce), it should and can be used sparingly—a little goes a long way.

Walnut oil has been used for other purposes besides cuisine. In ancient Egypt, it was used in embalming fluid to preserve mummies. Until the last century it was used to light the oil lamps of Southwestern France (but not the finest grade, which was reserved for the kitchen). It also served as a holy oil; it was a crime in Sarlat during the eighteenth century to poach walnuts designated for oil to be burned in front of the Holy Sacrament. Dating from the seventeenth century, the oil has been used in painting. The impressionists sometimes favored walnut oil as a medium for color, even though poppy and linseed oils, by then available, were considered superior for artistic use.

Moulin de la Tour
Moulin à eau du XVIᵉ siècle

FABRICATION ARTISANALE ET VENTE
D'HUILE VIERGE DE NOIX ET DE NOISETTE

VISITE DE LA FABRICATION TOUS LES VENDREDIS
PLUS LES LUNDIS ET MERCREDIS (JUILLET - AOÛT)

RENSEIGNEMENTS : TÉL. 53.59.22.08

SAINTE-NATHALÈNE EN PÉRIGORD
à 9 km de Sarlat ~ D 47

The old Walnut Mill in Sainte-Nathalene: making walnut oil.

Chemical analyses show traces of walnut oil in paintings by Monet, Pissarro, and Cézanne.

In the hamlet of Sainte-Nathalène, near Sarlat in the heart of old Périgord, visitors can watch walnut oil being pressed in the old manner at the Moulin de la Tour. The water-driven mill has been in continual use for generations, and its enormous grindstone is centuries old. The aroma emanating from the trough is heavenly.

IN OLD PÉRIGORD

Until World War II, it was common in Périgord to see "nut-cracking women" *(les dames dénoisilleuses)* going from village to village in the fall carrying the simple instruments of their profession: a wooden mallet, a straw basket, and a flat stone to place on their laps. In fine weather they would sit outside the doors of their clients and ply their trade. Experienced workers would shatter shells with a single, sure blow. The pleasant sound of cracking shells gave rise to the saying, "No part of the walnut is wasted, not even the sound when it breaks."

The nuts were carefully sorted by quality, size, and color. It was crucial to expose the kernel without damage, because a broken nut lost much of its market value. The categories of quality were *extra* for whole hemispheres that were white; *arlequins* (clowns) for whole hemispheres that were patchy in color; *les invalides* (wounded ones) for those that were chipped; and finally, at the bottom of the scale, *les brisures* (broken ones) for those that were in pieces.

Sorting was often left to later in the season when more time was available in farming communities. Then families, neighbors, and friends would gather to work together. These were times of celebration, often including a meal followed by singing or dancing to the accompaniment of a fiddle. Such occasions permitted young people to fraternize under the scrutiny of their parents, and marriages were arranged during these events.

Specialized songs were popular at the work table, such as "The Nut Cracking Song," which recounts a local custom. A suitor could signal his interest in a girl by slipping a tiny, round walnut into her shelling tray. This sport walnut, no bigger than a hazelnut, was called a *cacalou* or *cacalon* in the

DANS LA RUE
1075. Casseuse de Noix.

Shelling nuts in the street.

local dialect *(le patois)*. What the little nut lacked in market value, it made up for in romantic significance.

A familiar scene in the Dordogne.

THE NUT CRACKING SONG

Refrain:
With a ping and pang, a ping and pang, Get cracking on those nuts!

*I. Here's to the girls at table
Who are sighing for the boys.
Give them plenty of nuts to shell
And never mind the noise.*

*II. The girls have lost their patience
And now they can't keep track
Because we've slipped the cacalons
Into their trays to crack.*

*III. Here's to the health of our hostess
Who serves us new white wine
And here's to the songs and stories
That help us pass the time.*

*IV. When midnight comes we'll celebrate
With food and merry notes
And end with a dance to make the girls
Hike up their petticoats!*

LE LOT ILLUSTRÉ — 314. Dénoisillage

Cracking nuts in the region of the Lot.

We get a sense of these bygone days from old picture postcards of Périgord, which are available at outdoor flea markets in the region. Several are reproduced here.

BUYING & PREPARING WALNUTS

Today's cook need not worry about locating whole pristine walnuts; broken pieces work just as well in these recipes, except perhaps for decorative touches. Cup measures given here were taken with walnuts bought as halves. Any kind of walnut will do, but to ensure freshness, we recommend buying shelled walnuts out of the bin in a grocery or natural foods store, rather than in commercial packages. Chopped walnuts are readily available in cellophane packages and are usually fine if consumed within one year. However, walnuts will go stale if stored too long in plastic. We recommend lightly toasting shelled walnuts before using them in any recipe, to bring out their flavor and enhance their taste.

Walnuts can be chopped, either coarsely or finely, by hand using a knife as the recipe indicates. A food processor makes the job easier. To chop coarsely, grind in short bursts and watch to make sure that the nuts are not chopped too finely. To reduce the nuts to a powder, leave the processor on and watch carefully so that the mass does not become gummy. If the machine has a fine grating blade, use it for reducing walnuts to powder.

RECIPE SUBSTITUTIONS

Some of these recipes call for local ingredients that are not readily available outside France, but substitutions are possible. In the category of spirits, *vin de noix* is a strong, semisweet apéritif that often appears in traditional walnut recipes but is rarely found in the United States. You might try making *vin de noix* from scratch, using the recipe given in the section entitled "Liqueurs and Spirits." An alternative is to substitute sweet vermouth warmed with walnuts.

> *1 cup sweet vermouth*
>
> *¼ cup walnuts*

Warm the mixture. Let it sit for 30 minutes, then strain through a colander, discarding the walnuts.

To substitute for walnut liqueur, which is not the same as *vin de noix,* use any commercial nut liqueur, such as amaretto, almond brandy, or crème de noisette or another hazelnut liqueur.

Fresh spices are always better than their dry varieties. If a recipe calls for several spices and one is not available, proceed using only those at hand. The resulting dish is usually just as delicious, if a little different from the intended dish. Dried spices are stronger than their fresh counterparts. To substitute dried for fresh spices, use ⅛ to ¼ of the quantity recommended.

For individuals who have trouble digesting garlic, shallots may be substituted in any recipe. Similarly, any fresh mushroom may be substituted for wild mushrooms such as morels, which may be featured as ingredients.

Finally, the French use a number of dairy products for which there is no exact substitute. Crème fraîche can be made at home using the following recipe.

> *1 teaspoon buttermilk*
>
> *1 cup heavy cream*

Pour the cream into a glass jar. Stir in the buttermilk. Cover the jar loosely with a lid or plastic wrap. Let the mixture stand in a warm spot for 6 to 24 hours. Stir. Then cover tightly with a lid or plastic wrap, and store in the refrigerator. To substitute for crème fraîche, use heavy cream in dishes that require cooking or plain yogurt in dishes that do not.

Fromage blanc is a fresh skim-milk cheese. Plain yogurt makes a good substitute in uncooked dishes. Heavy cream can often substitute in cooked dishes.

Bleu d'Auvergne and Roquefort are called for in a number of these recipes. Each has a distinctive taste, but another mild blue cheese, such as Danish blue cheese, can be substituted with good results. Stronger blue cheeses can overwhelm the blend of other ingredients in a recipe; in most cases Roquefort is preferable.

Substitutions do not necessarily mean compromises; rather, they are opportunities for experiment. These recipes are best executed with a free hand. Except for cakes and breads, quantities of ingredients can be varied according to taste. The same is true for pan sizes. Feel free to use your favorite pans and methods for coating them and removing contents.

Jean-Luc Toussaint is an extremely inventive cook who delights in utilizing whatever is at hand in the cupboard—good advice for the American cook, too. We join him in wishing you many happy hours in the kitchen and at table. As Jean-Luc exhorts his French readers: *"Alors, au travail et bon appétit!"*

Appetizers and Hors d'Oeuvres

LES AMUSE-GUEULE ET LES PETITS HORS D'OEUVRE

Prunes Stuffed with Apples and Walnuts

Roquefort-Walnut Toasts

Avocado-Walnut Toasts

Tartlets with Blue Cheese and Walnuts

Toasted Salted Walnuts

Warm Walnut and Meat Pastries

Smoked Duck Rolls

Prunes Stuffed with Apples and Walnuts

Walnut Tapenade

Roquefort-Walnut Toasts

Canapés à la Crème de Roquefort

SERVES 12 (36 TOASTS)

> 18 thin slices of loaf rye bread, or 36 appetizer-size slices,
>   lightly toasted
>
> 1 ¼ cups walnut pieces, including 18 unbroken walnut halves
>
> 2 ½ cups (14 ounces) crumbled Roquefort cheese
>
> 6 tablespoons unsalted butter, softened
>
> 2 tablespoons Armagnac or other brandy
>
> 9 cherry tomatoes, cut in half
>
> 2 tablespoons minced chives, for garnish

1. Cut the toasted bread into 36 rounds, triangles, or squares.

2. Set aside 18 of the best walnut halves. Place remaining walnut pieces in the bowl of a food processor and reduce to a powder (be careful not to let it become paste). Add Roquefort cheese, softened butter, and brandy. Pulse until creamy and smooth.

3. Spread each toast with Roquefort cream. Decorate 18 of the toasts with walnut halves and the remaining 18 with cherry tomato halves. Sprinkle each with a pinch of minced chives.

4. Arrange the toasts on a platter and serve.

Avocado-Walnut Toasts

Crème d'Avocat sur Canapés

SERVES 6 (12 TOASTS)

1 cup walnut pieces, including 12 unbroken halves

2 ripe avocados

1 tablespoon lemon juice

2 tablespoons plain yogurt

1 teaspoon acacia honey or other type of honey

Pinch of ground coriander

Freshly ground pepper to taste

12 slices of loaf rye bread, lightly toasted

1. Set aside 12 unbroken walnut halves. Place the remaining walnut pieces in the bowl of a food processor. Process on medium speed about 8 seconds. Add meat of the avocado, lemon juice, yogurt, and honey. Season with a pinch of coriander. Process until smooth. Add salt and pepper to taste.

2. Cut the toasted bread slices into 12 rounds or other decorative shapes. Spread the avocado cream onto the toasts.

3. Decorate each with a walnut half and serve.

Tartlets with Blue Cheese and Walnuts

Tartelettes au Bleu et aux Noix

SERVES 6 (12 TARTLETS)

1 double-crust tart dough (or double the recipe for Pâte Brisée *on page 132)*

2 tablespoons unsalted butter

2 small shallots, finely minced

1 ¼ cups walnut pieces

1 ¼ cups (7 ounces) crumbled Bleu d'Auvergne cheese, including 12 unbroken halves

6 tablespoons crème fraîche, or 4 tablespoons heavy cream

1 tablespoon Cognac or other brandy

Freshly ground pepper

1. Preheat oven to 400°.

2. Dust a flat surface with flour, and roll out the pastry into a thin (⅛ inch) sheet. Cut the pastry into 12 pieces and line in 12 tartlet pans, small pastry molds, or shallow muffin pans. Press the dough lightly into the pan. Trim off excess dough, leaving ⅛ inch extending above the pan rim. Flute the rims with the dull edge of a knife and prick the bottom of the dough with a fork. Place the prepared pans in the freezer for a minimum of 15 minutes (they can remain in the freezer in an airtight container for up to 3 months).

3. Place the pans directly on middle oven rack, and bake the shells for 5 to 8 minutes, or until they begin to turn golden.

4. Meanwhile, warm the butter in a small frying pan over medium heat. Add the finely minced shallots and cook until the shallots become translucent

—22—

and have absorbed most of the butter. Do not brown. Remove the pan from the heat and let stand to cool. Add pepper to taste.

5. Remove the tartlet pans from the oven and turn the heat down to 350°.

6. Set aside 12 unbroken walnut halves. Place remaining walnuts in the bowl of a food processor, and chop to a fine consistency. Add Bleu d'Auvergne, crème fraîche, and Cognac, and mix until smooth.

7. In each pastry shell, place a portion of cooked shallots, then the cheese-nut cream. Decorate each with a walnut half. Return to the oven for 10 to 15 minutes.

8. Let the tartlets cool slightly, and gently remove each tartlet from its pan. (Do not refrigerate, since that will make shells soggy.) When ready to serve, reheat the pastries on a baking sheet in the oven at 350°.

Toasted Salted Walnuts

Noix Salées

SERVES 6

2 tablespoons peanut oil

2 tablespoons unsalted butter

2 cups walnut halves

Salt

1. Heat the oil and butter in a frying pan on medium heat. Add the walnuts and sauté lightly, shaking the pan continuously until the nuts are golden brown.

2. Using a slotted spoon, transfer the walnuts from the pan onto paper towels. Let them drain a bit. Then, while still warm, add salt to taste.

3. Serve warm or at room temperature in a small bowl.

Warm Walnut and Meat Pastries

Petits Friands aux Noix

SERVES 6 (12 PASTRIES)

16 ounces puff pastry (ready-made frozen sheets or your own recipe)

½ pound lean ground beef or ground turkey

3 tablespoons chopped fresh basil, or 1 teaspoon dried

½ cup walnut pieces, coarsely chopped

1 tablespoon minced shallots

1 whole egg

2 tablespoons heavy cream

Salt and freshly ground pepper

1 egg yolk

1. Thaw frozen puff pastry according to package directions, or prepare your own puff pastry. Preheat oven to 400°.

2. In a bowl, mix together the ground beef, chopped basil, chopped nuts, minced shallots, 1 whole egg, and cream. When well mixed, add salt and pepper to taste.

3. Spread or roll out the puff pastry sheets, and cut them into 12 squares.

4. Place a spoonful of the meat mixture on each pastry square, dividing the mixture equally among them. Fold the pastry over into a triangle, and pinch the open edges closed with a fork.

5. Beat the egg yolk with a few drops of water and use a pastry brush to glaze each pastry with egg yolk.

6. Put the pastries on a baking sheet and bake about 12 minutes, or until golden brown. Serve warm.

Prunes Stuffed with Apples and Walnuts

Pruneaux Farcis aux Pommes et Noix

SERVES 6 (18 APPETIZERS)

3 apples

4 tablespoons butter

3 tablespoons Calvados, apple brandy, or other brandy

¼ cup walnut pieces, finely chopped

18 pitted prunes (if not stored in liquid, soak 1 hour in warm water)

18 thin slices bacon

1. Peel, core, and finely dice the apples.

2. Melt the butter over medium-low heat, add diced apples, and cook gently without browning. When apples have softened, add the Calvados and the finely chopped walnuts. Stir to mix evenly.

3. Fill the hollow of each prune with the apple-nut mixture. Wrap a slice of bacon around each prune and secure with a toothpick.

4. Just before serving, cook the prunes in a 425° oven for 6 to 8 minutes, or until the bacon is crisp.

5. Serve the stuffed prunes warm, on a platter.

Smoked Duck Rolls

Roulades de Magret Fumé

SERVES 6 (12 ROLLS)

18 fresh leaves of lemon balm (lemon mint) or other mint

1 cup walnut pieces, including 12 unbroken halves

4 ounces fromage blanc or plain yogurt

2 tablespoons walnut liqueur (liqueur de noix) or other nut liqueur such as amaretto or crème de noisette

Pinch of cayenne pepper

Salt

12 slices smoked duck breast (magret de canard fumé)

1 melon, thinly sliced

1. Set aside 12 leaves of lemon balm. Finely mince the remaining 6 leaves by hand and place them in a mixing bowl.

2. Set aside 12 unbroken walnut halves. Finely chop the remaining walnuts and add them to the minced leaves.

3. Add fromage blanc, liqueur, and cayenne. Stir to mix well. Add salt to taste.

4. Spread a portion of the nut mix on each slice of smoked duck. Roll up each slice to form a cylinder (roulade). The roulades may be chilled for several hours, but allow time for them to return to room temperature before serving.

5. On each plate, place two roulades, several melon slices, 2 walnut halves, and two mint leaves. Serve as an opening course.

Walnut Tapenade

Tapenoix

SERVES 6

Freshly squeezed juice of 1 lemon

1 tablespoon prepared Dijon mustard

4 tablespoons olive oil

¾ cup walnut pieces

¾ cup pitted green olives

¾ cup pitted black olives

12 anchovy fillets

2 tablespoons capers

6 slices wheat bread

1. Mix together the lemon juice, mustard, and olive oil in a bowl.

2. In a food processor, blend the walnuts, green and black olives, anchovy fillets, and capers. With the motor running, incorporate the oil mixture in a thin stream. Chill at least 15 minutes in the refrigerator.

3. Shortly before serving, toast the slices of wheat bread, and cut them into 12 rounds or triangles.

4. Spread the chilled olive paste on the toast and serve.

Sauces

LES SAUCES

Walnut products: vinegar, oil, salad dressing, and mustard.

Walnut Vinaigrette Sauce

Garlic-Walnut Sauce

Walnut-Oil Mayonnaise

Horseradish and Walnut Sauce

Walnut Vinaigrette Sauce

Sauce Vinaigrette au Noix

MAKES ⅓ CUP

> ½ cup walnut pieces
>
> 2 tablespoons safflower oil or other mild vegetable oil
>
> 1 tablespoon walnut oil
>
> 1 tablespoon raspberry vinegar
>
> Pinch each of salt and freshly ground pepper

In the bowl of a food processor, reduce the walnuts to a powder. Add the safflower oil, walnut oil, vinegar, salt, and pepper. Process until the sauce is smooth.

Garlic-Walnut Sauce

Aillade aux Noix

MAKES ⅔ TO ¾ CUP

> ½ cup walnut pieces
>
> 6 cloves garlic, peeled
>
> ¼ cup walnut oil
>
> Salt and freshly ground pepper

Place the walnuts and peeled garlic cloves in the bowl of a food processor and mix to a paste. Little by little, add the walnut oil to the mixture in the food processor, pulsing to mix until you have a smooth mayonnaise-like sauce. (Purists would not use the food processor for this last step but would whip the mixture with a fork.) Add salt and pepper to taste.

Walnut-Oil Mayonnaise

Mayonnaise à l'Huile de Noix

MAKES ⅓ CUP

1 small garlic clove, peeled

1 egg yolk

¼ teaspoon prepared Dijon mustard

¼ cup walnut oil

Salt and freshly ground pepper

Crush the garlic clove. Place in a bowl with the egg yolk and mustard, and beat with a wire whip. Continue beating and add the walnut oil slowly in a fine thread until mixture thickens. Add salt and pepper to taste.

Horseradish and Walnut Sauce

Sauce Raifort aux Noix

Serve this sauce as an accompaniment to trout or a cold fillet of salmon.

MAKES 2 ½ CUPS

1 cup walnut pieces

1 cup grated horseradish

2 teaspoons sugar

⅔ cup crème fraîche or plain yogurt

Pinch of salt

In the bowl of a food processor, pulse walnuts almost to a powder. In a bowl, mix together the powdered walnuts, grated horseradish, sugar, crème fraîche, and salt.

Salads

LES SALADES

Chicken Salad with Avocados

Celeriac, Apple, and Walnut Salad

Artichoke Hearts with Blue Cheese and Walnuts

Roasted Onion, Rice, and Walnut Salad

Autumn Salad

Coleslaw with Blue Cheese and Walnuts

Duck Salad with Cherries and Walnuts

Fresh Fig Salad with Walnuts

Chicken Liver Salad with Apples and Grapes

Chicken Salad with Avocados

Salad Surprise with Yogurt

Smoked Trout Salad with Avocados and Walnuts

Escarole with Walnuts and Truffles

Celeriac, Apple, and Walnut Salad

Céleri-Rave, Pommes et Noix en Salade

SERVES 6

1 small celeriac (celery root), peeled

1 small head of Batavia lettuce, or endive or escarole

1 cup walnut pieces

2 Granny Smith apples

*$1/2$ to $3/4$ cup Walnut-Oil Mayonnaise (see page 31)
or regular mayonnaise*

1 tablespoon crème fraîche or plain yogurt

1 tablespoon chopped fresh chives

1 tablespoon chopped fresh parsley

1 tablespoon chopped fresh chervil

1. Bring water to boil in a large pot. Reduce heat and simmer the celeriac for 15 minutes. Drain and refrigerate.

2. Wash, drain, and dry the Batavia.

3. Coarsely chop the walnuts and set aside.

4. When the celeriac is cool, dice it finely. (While waiting for the celeriac to cool, you can make the Walnut Mayonnaise.)

5. Wash the apples, and without peeling them, core and cut them into thin slices.

6. In a bowl, combine the mayonnaise, crème fraîche, and herbs. Add the apple slices and the diced celeriac, and mix well.

7. Arrange a bed of salad greens on a salad dish or shallow bowl. Top the greens with the apple-celeriac mix. Sprinkle with chopped walnuts. Serve chilled.

Artichoke Hearts with Blue Cheese and Walnuts

Fonds d'Artichauts au Bleu et aux Noix

SERVES 6

Salad

1 large or 2 small heads of mache (lamb's lettuce or corn salad)
or other loose-leaf lettuce

1 small green bell pepper

6 artichoke hearts, canned, bottled, or freshly cooked

2 tablespoons chopped chives

Sauce

1 cup walnut pieces

3/4 cup (4 ounces) crumbled Bleu d'Auvergne or other mild blue cheese

1 tablespoon Cognac or other brandy

Freshly squeezed juice of 1/2 lemon

5 tablespoons walnut oil

1. Wash, drain, and dry the mache. Wash and dry the green pepper. Remove top, stem, membranes, and seeds. Slice flesh into thin strips. Rinse and drain the artichoke hearts. Set these vegetables aside.

2. Prepare the sauce: In the bowl of a food processor, finely chop the walnuts. Add the Bleu d'Auvergne, Cognac, and lemon juice, and pulse. While mixing continuously, add the oil in a thin thread until sauce is smooth.

3. Place the lettuce leaves, artichoke hearts, and green peppers in a salad bowl. Sprinkle with chopped chives. Pour the sauce decoratively over the salad. Serve immediately.

Roasted Onion, Rice, and Walnut Salad

Oignons Cuits en Salade et aux Noix

Salad

1¾ *pounds yellow onions*

1 *cup cooked long-grained rice, cooled and fluffed*

½ *teaspoon salt*

1 *cup walnut pieces, coarsely chopped*

2 *tablespoons chopped chives, for garnish*

Vinaigrette

3 *tablespoons walnut oil*

1 *tablespoon peanut oil*

2 *tablespoons raspberry vinegar*

Salt and freshly ground pepper

1. Preheat oven to 350°.

2. Without peeling them, place the onions on a baking sheet or in a roasting pan and cook for 1 hour.

3. When the onions are cooked through, remove them from the oven and allow to cool. Peel them and cut each in half.

4. Make a vinaigrette by whisking together the two oils, raspberry vinegar, and salt and pepper to taste.

5. Form a dome of cooled, fluffed rice in the middle of a serving platter. Surround the rice with onion halves. Moisten the rice and onions with the vinaigrette. Sprinkle liberally with chopped walnuts and chopped chives to garnish. Serve at room temperature.

Autumn Salad

Salade d'Automne

Salad

1 head romaine, rocket, or other firm lettuce

3 small wild mushrooms (chanterelles, morels, shiitakes, or portobellos)

2 pears

Freshly squeezed juice of 1 lemon

1 cup (4 ounces) Edam or Gouda cheese

1 cup walnut pieces, coarsely chopped

Vinaigrette

Freshly squeezed juice of 1 lemon

2 tablespoons walnut oil

1 tablespoon peanut oil

1 tablespoon sherry vinegar or balsamic vinegar

½ teaspoon prepared Dijon mustard

Salt and freshly ground pepper

1. Separate the lettuce leaves from their root and discard the root. Wash the leaves, drain them, and set them aside to dry.

2. Clean the mushrooms and wash the pears. Cut both into fine matchstick pieces. Moisten with the lemon juice to prevent browning.

3. Cut the cheese into fine matchstick pieces.

4. Place a bed of lettuce on each plate. Sprinkle with a portion of the pears, mushrooms, cheese, and chopped walnuts.

5. Make a vinaigrette by whipping together the lemon juice, walnut oil, peanut oil, vinegar, mustard, and salt and pepper to taste. Sprinkle each salad with a portion of the vinaigrette.

Coleslaw with Blue Cheese and Walnuts

Salade de Choucroute au Bleu et aux Noix

SERVES 6

> 1 head of cabbage, white or red, or Chinese cabbage or bok choy
>
> 1¼ cups walnut halves, including 6 unbroken halves
>
> ¾ cup (4 ounces) crumbled Bleu d'Auvergne or other mild blue cheese
>
> ½ cup crème fraîche or sour cream
>
> Freshly squeezed juice of 1 lemon
>
> Pinch of freshly ground pepper
>
> 3 tablespoons chives, chopped
>
> 3 tablespoons fresh chervil, chopped

1. Soak the cabbage in cold water for 10 minutes. Rinse, drain well, and press water out with a cloth or paper towel. Allow to continue drying on a rack, upside down.

2. Set aside six unbroken walnut halves. Put the remaining walnuts in the bowl of a food processor and chop finely. Add blue cheese, crème fraîche, juice of 1 lemon, pinch of freshly ground pepper, half the chives, and half the chervil. Blend to a smooth sauce. Pour into a container and refrigerate.

3. Remove the core from the cabbage. Using the coarse grating blade of the food processor, shred the cabbage leaves. (If you prefer, chop the cabbage by hand.) Chill.

4. Just before serving, dress the shredded cabbage with the sauce. Sprinkle with the remaining chopped chives and chopped chervil. Decorate with the walnut halves. Serve chilled.

Duck Salad with Cherries and Walnuts

Salade de Confit de Canard aux Cerises et aux Noix

SERVES 6

Salad

1 head firm lettuce (Batavia, endive, escarole, or romaine)

1¼ pounds cherries

3 preserved duck thighs (canned or bottled)

1¼ cups walnut pieces, coarsely chopped

3 small green onions, coarsely chopped

3 tablespoons chopped chives

Salt and freshly ground pepper

Vinaigrette

3 tablespoons walnut oil

2 tablespoons safflower oil or other mild vegetable oil

3 tablespoons raspberry vinegar

1. Preheat oven to 350°. Wash, drain, and dry the lettuce. Rinse the cherries and remove the pits and stems.

2. Drain the duck thighs and put them in a roasting pan. Roast in the oven for 15 minutes. Remove from oven and let cool until comfortable to handle.

3. Meanwhile, make a vinaigrette by whisking together the two oils and the raspberry vinegar. Set aside.

4. Remove the skin and bones from the duck. Cut the meat into thin strips.

5. Place a bed of lettuce on each plate. Top with duck meat (still warm), chopped walnuts, chopped onions, and pitted cherries. Sprinkle with chopped chives. Season each salad with vinaigrette, salt, and pepper to taste. Serve immediately.

Fresh Fig Salad with Walnuts

Salade de Figues Fraîches aux Noix

SERVES 6

Salad

1 head green lettuce

¾ pound fresh, ripe (soft) figs

12 thin slices smoked duck breast (magret de canard fumé)

1¼ cups walnut pieces, coarsely chopped

Sauce

½ cup crème fraîche or plain yogurt

3 tablespoons raspberry vinegar

Freshly squeezed juice of 1 lemon

Salt and freshly ground pepper

1 teaspoon chopped chives

1 teaspoon finely chopped fresh chervil

1 teaspoon finely chopped fresh parsley

1. Wash, drain, and dry the lettuce, discarding any wilted outer leaves. Wash the figs and remove the stems. Cut each fig in quarters. Cut each duck slice in two.

2. Prepare the sauce by mixing the crème fraîche, vinegar, lemon juice, a sprinkling of salt and pepper, and the fresh chopped herbs.

3. Line the bottom of a shallow salad bowl with the lettuce leaves. Arrange the duck slices, cut figs, and chopped walnuts on top.

4. Serve salad chilled, dressed with the sauce.

Chicken Liver Salad with Apples and Grapes

Salade de Foies de Volaille aux Pommes et Raisins

SERVES 6

Salad

4 Granny Smith apples

1 head mache (lamb's lettuce or corn salad) or other loose-leaf lettuce

1 bunch green seedless grapes

1 pound chicken livers

2 teaspoons unsalted butter

¾ cup walnut pieces, coarsely chopped

Vinaigrette

3 tablespoons walnut oil

1 tablespoon raspberry vinegar

1 teaspoon finely chopped fresh parsley

Salt and freshly ground pepper

1. Wash and core the apples. Don't peel them. Cut the apples into thin slices. Wash the mache carefully, drain, and dry. Pick the grapes off their stems, peel them, and if they are not seedless, remove the seeds. Set aside.

2. Clean the chicken livers and mince them. Over medium-high heat, bring the butter to a foam and quickly sauté the minced chicken livers. Turn them into a strainer and let drain.

3. Make a vinaigrette by whisking together the walnut oil, vinegar, chopped parsley, and a sprinkling of salt and pepper.

4. Place a bed of lettuce on each plate. Add a portion of warm chicken livers and apple slices. Dress each salad with vinaigrette and top with the peeled grapes and chopped walnuts. Serve immediately.

Chicken Salad with Avocados

Salade de Poulet à l'Avocat

SERVES 6

Salad

6 chicken breast halves, skinned and boned

1 tablespoon safflower oil or other mild vegetable oil

Salt and freshly ground pepper

½ pound mushrooms

Freshly squeezed juice of 1 lemon

2 avocados

1 cup walnut pieces, including 12 unbroken halves

3 shallots, peeled and finely chopped

Vinaigrette

3 tablespoons walnut oil

1 tablespoon white wine vinegar

1 teaspoon minced fresh parsley

Salt and freshly ground pepper

1. Sauté the chicken breasts in the safflower oil over medium heat for about 6 minutes per side. Add salt and pepper to taste. Allow to cool.

2. Wash, dry, and thinly slice the mushrooms. Sprinkle with half the lemon juice. Peel and thinly slice avocados, and sprinkle with remaining lemon juice. Set aside 12 walnut halves and coarsely chop the remaining walnuts.

3. Prepare a vinaigrette by whisking together the walnut oil, vinegar, minced parsley, and a sprinkling of salt and pepper.

4. When chicken breasts are cool, cut them lengthwise into ¼-inch slices.

5. Arrange slices of chicken, mushroom, and avocado on each plate. Sprinkle with chopped shallots and vinaigrette. Decorate with walnut halves.

Salad Surprise with Yogurt

Salade Surprise au Yaourt

SERVES 6

1 head celery (at least 6 stalks)

1 Granny Smith apple

Freshly squeezed juice of ½ lemon

3 clementines (red tangerines) or blood oranges

1 grapefruit

1 cup walnut pieces

1 cup plain yogurt

Pinch of cumin

Pinch of grated fresh ginger

Salt and freshly ground pepper

1. Cut the ends off the celery stalks. Discard any outer stalks that are really tough. Use a vegetable peeler to scrape off the fibrous outer skin of each branch. Wash and drain the scraped branches and cut them crosswise into thin slices. Set aside in a salad bowl.

2. Peel, core, and dice the apple. Moisten the diced apple with lemon juice. Peel the clementines and the grapefruit, taking care to remove all the rind and membranes. Finely chop the walnuts.

3. Add the fruits and walnuts to the celery slices. Combine the yogurt, cumin, ginger, and a sprinkling of salt and pepper. Mix well. Add to the salad and toss well.

4. Chill and serve cool.

Smoked Trout Salad with Avocados and Walnuts

Salade de Truite Fumée à l'Avocat et aux Noix

SERVES 6

- *3 avocados*
- *1 cup walnut pieces*
- *3 tablespoons walnut oil*
- *3 lemons*
- *Salt and freshly ground pepper*
- *6 smoked trout fillets*
- *2 tablespoons chopped chives*
- *6 sprigs parsley*

1. Peel avocados, remove the pits, and cut the flesh into thin slices.

2. In the bowl of a food processor, chop the walnuts. Add walnut oil and juice of 2 of the lemons, and mix until smooth. Add salt and pepper to taste.

3. Cut remaining lemon into six slices. On each plate, place a portion of avocado slices and season with the walnut sauce. Place a trout fillet on each bed of avocados. Sprinkle with a pinch of chopped chives. Garnish each plate with a slice of lemon and a sprig of parsley. Serve cool.

Escarole with Walnuts and Truffles

Scarole aux Noix et à la Truffe

SERVES 6

Salad

1 head escarole lettuce

1 small truffle

1 cup walnut pieces

Salt and freshly ground pepper

Vinaigrette

2 tablespoons sherry vinegar

4 tablespoons walnut oil

Pinch each of salt and freshly ground pepper

1. Wash the escarole, removing any wilted outer leaves. Drain and dry. Wipe the truffle clean and cut it into thin matchsticks. Chop and crush the walnuts coarsely.

2. Make a vinaigrette by whisking together the sherry vinegar, walnut oil, and salt and pepper.

3. Tear the escarole into bite-sized pieces and place in a salad bowl. Salt and pepper the lettuce, add the vinaigrette, and toss well. Top with the truffle sticks and crushed walnuts. Serve immediately.

Warm and Cold Entrées

LES ENTRÉES CHAUDES ET FROIDES

Marinated Goat Cheese Rounds

Olive Bread with Ham

Grated Carrots with Raisins and Walnuts

Cucumber Salad with Walnut-Yogurt Dressing

Crêpes Filled with Cheese and Walnuts

Crusted Duck Pâté with Prunes and Walnuts

Country Meat Pâté with Walnuts

Walnut Quenelles (Dumplings)

Roquefort-Walnut Quiche

Stuffed Spanish Mussels

Autumn Quiche with Walnuts

Roquefort-Walnut Omelet

Rabbit Terrine

Chicken Liver Terrine

Marinated Goat Cheese Rounds

Cabécous à l'Huile de Noix

SERVES 6

This recipe takes one week to prepare. Feel free to make substitutions. If the traditional *cabécou* form of goat cheese is not available, make rounds from any goat cheese you can find. Also, use whatever herbs are fresh and savory. It is fine to use 7 sprigs of one type of herb for the entire jar if a variety is not available. If you run out of walnut oil, substitute olive oil.

3 sprigs thyme

6 small semidry goat-cheese rounds (cabécous)

2 sprigs basil

1 sprig savory

1 sprig rosemary

18 or more peppercorns

1 bay leaf

Walnut oil to cover cheese

1 clove garlic (optional)

1. Place a sprig of thyme on the bottom of a large jar. Stack the goat-cheese rounds in the jar with 1 sprig of one of the herbs and 3 or more peppercorns on top of each cheese round. Slide the bay leaf into the jar on the side. (If you like a strong garlic taste, add a clove of garlic.) Fill the jar with walnut oil to cover cheese and close the jar firmly.

2. Store in a cool, dark place for at least a week. The longer you marinate the cheese, the more savory it will be.

3. When ready to serve, drain the cheese lightly, reserving the walnut oil for use in salad dressings. Serve each cheese round on a slice of toasted firm bread—rye, whole wheat, or farmer's. May also be accompanied with a green salad, dressed with walnut oil, and garnished with walnut pieces.

Olive Bread with Ham

Cake aux Olives au Jambon

SERVES 6

4 eggs

⅓ cup vegetable oil

⅔ cup milk

Salt and freshly ground pepper

1½ cups flour

2¼ teaspoons baking powder

5 ounces pitted green olives

1¼ cups walnut pieces, chopped very coarsely

4 ounces ham, diced

1¼ cups (5 ounces) grated French Comté or other mild firm cheese such
   as Cantal, Gruyère, or Swiss

1 tablespoon unsalted butter

1. Preheat oven to 350°. Butter a 9-inch round cake pan or standard loaf pan.

2. In a large bowl, beat the eggs with a wire whip until well mixed and foamy. Add the oil, milk, and a sprinkle of salt and pepper. Sift flour and baking powder together. Gradually add to the egg mixture. Beat with a spoon until all ingredients are incorporated. Do not overmix.

3. Drain the olives well and incorporate them into the dough along with the walnuts, diced ham, and grated cheese. Turn the dough into the cake pan.

4. Bake 1 hour and 15 minutes, or until an inserted knife comes clean.

5. Remove bread from oven. Place on cooling rack for 8 to 10 minutes until slightly cool. Turn the loaf out of the pan. Slice and serve warm.

Note: This bread is dense and thus excellent for picnics or for packed lunches.

Grated Carrots with Raisins and Walnuts

Carottes Râpées aux Raisins Secs et aux Noix

SERVES 6

2 pounds carrots, washed, peeled, and with ends cut off

Freshly squeezed juice of 1 lemon

2 tablespoons walnut oil

1 tablespoon peanut oil

Salt and freshly ground pepper

3 tablespoons minced fresh parsley

¾ cup walnut pieces, coarsely chopped

¾ cup raisins

1. Grate or shred the peeled carrots using a food processor or a coarse hand grater.

2. In a bowl, prepare a vinaigrette by mixing the lemon juice and the two oils well with a fork or wire whip. Add salt and pepper to taste.

3. Place the shredded carrots in a serving bowl, pour the vinaigrette over the carrots, and toss well.

4. Decorate the tossed carrots with the minced parsley, chopped walnuts, and raisins.

5. Chill. Serve cold.

Cucumber Salad with Walnut-Yogurt Dressing

Concombre et Lait Caillé aux Noix

SERVES 6

1 large cucumber or several small ones

2 cloves garlic

1 cup walnut pieces, finely minced

Salt

2 cups plain yogurt

1 to 3 tablespoons minced fresh mint

2 teaspoons olive oil (optional)

1. Peel the cucumber and dice small. Arrange the diced cucumber on paper towels, salt, and allow to drain.

2. Crush the garlic cloves, remove peels, sprinkle liberally with salt, and crush the peeled garlic again, very well. Add crushed garlic and minced walnuts to the yogurt, and stir until blended.

3. Arrange the drained cucumber on a serving plate and spoon the walnut cream over it. Sprinkle with minced mint. Drizzle a thread of olive oil over the top.

4. Chill. Serve cold.

Crêpes Filled with Cheese and Walnuts

Crêpes Fourrées au Fromage et aux Noix

SERVES 6 (12 CRÊPES)

Batter

1 cup flour

2 to 3 pinches of salt

2 eggs

1⅓ cups milk

Pinch of sugar

Filling

1 clove garlic, peeled

½ cup dry white wine

*4 cups (14 ounces) grated French Comté or another mild firm cheese
  such as Cantal, Gruyère, or Swiss*

1 teaspoon kirsch or other cherry brandy

¾ cup walnut pieces

3 tablespoons unsalted butter

1 onion, finely chopped

3 ounces mushrooms, finely minced

4 ounces ham, coarsely diced

¼ cup vegetable oil

1. Prepare the crêpe batter: Sift the flour into a large bowl. Add salt, eggs, half the milk, and the sugar. Beat with a wire whip until the batter is smooth. Add the remaining milk, mix, and let sit for 1 hour.

2. Meanwhile, prepare the filling: Rub a saucepan with the garlic clove. Add the white wine. Warm over medium heat. When wine simmers, add 3 cups of the grated cheese and stir until smooth and well blended. Add the kirsch. Remove from heat, cover, and keep warm.

3. In a frying pan, heat 1 tablespoon of butter and sauté the onion in the butter for 2 minutes. Add the finely chopped mushrooms and cook another minute. Add diced ham and half the finely chopped walnuts, and cook 1 minute.

4. Now prepare the crêpes: Preheat oven to 400°. Butter a shallow ovenproof casserole dish.

5. Melt 2 tablespoons of butter, add it to the crêpe batter, and stir gently.

6. Brush a 7-inch crêpe pan or skillet with vegetable oil. Heat the pan over medium-high heat until the oil begins to smoke. Remove the pan from the flame, and quickly pour ¼ cup of batter into the middle of the pan. Tilt the pan back and forth quickly to cover the pan with a thin layer of batter. Return to the heat, and cook 1 minute. Shake the pan to loosen the crêpe. Lift the crêpe with a spatula, checking that it is lightly browned and ready for turning. Flip the crêpe over and brown lightly for about 30 seconds. Slide the crêpe onto a plate. Brush the skillet with oil again, and repeat until all the batter is used, making about 12 crêpes in all.

7. Put a portion of melted cheese on each crêpe. Top with the onion-walnut filling, and roll the crêpes up. Place the filled crêpes in the shallow baking dish and sprinkle the rest of the cheese and the remaining chopped walnuts. Warm in the oven for 5 minutes before serving.

Crusted Duck Pâté with Prunes and Walnuts

Pâté de Canard aux Pruneaux et aux Noix

SERVES 6

The pastry should be made the day before so it can rest overnight. If you're in a hurry, let it rest at least 2 hours before cooking. Another short-cut is to ask your butcher to skin, bone, and chop the duck meat so you can skip the treatment of the duck in steps 2 and 6.

Crust

5 cups flour

2 teaspoons salt

13 tablespoons chilled unsalted butter, cut into ½-inch slices

Up to 1 cup chilled water

Filling

1 duck (3 pounds or more)

2 tablespoons vegetable oil

1¼ cups pitted prunes

1¾ cups dry red wine

1 cup walnut pieces, coarsely chopped

Salt and freshly ground pepper

1. Start the pastry the night before. Sift the flour with the salt and place in the bowl of a food processor, along with the chilled butter and ¼ cup of the water. Process quickly, adding more tablespoons of water as needed to enable the dough to pull together into a ball. Remove the dough from the oven, form into a ball, cover with a thin cloth or plastic wrap, and leave in the refrigerator overnight (or at least 2 hours).

2. The next day (or when you are ready to start cooking), remove the dough from the refrigerator and allow to warm slightly. It will need to be just under room temperature to be workable. Heat the oil in a deep frying pan or heavy casserole. Brown the duck on all sides. Remove and allow to cool.

3. Simmer the pitted prunes 20 minutes in the red wine. Allow to cool in the wine. (When cool, drain the prunes, reserving the wine for deglazing a meat pan on another day.)

4. Preheat oven to 425°. Grease a mold or loaf pan.

5. Roll the dough out to a rectangle of ⅛-inch thickness. Plan the shape so that you will have a smaller piece big enough to cover the top of the mold and a larger piece big enough to line the mold completely. Cut the pastry into these two pieces. Lower the larger piece into the mold. Lightly press it into the bottom and corners. Trim the edges of the pastry, leaving a ¼-inch rim.

6. Remove and discard the skin of the duck (or save the skin to cut up and toss with a salad as duck cracklings). Bone the duck and chop the meat coarsely. Add salt and pepper to taste.

7. Place half the chopped duck meat on the pastry in the mold in an even layer. Add a layer of all the prunes (well drained), then cover with all the chopped walnuts. Finish with the remaining duck meat. Cover the top with the second pastry sheet. Pinch or flute the pastry ends together. Brush the exposed pastry with beaten egg yolk. Prick the pastry a few times with a fork.

8. Cook 50 minutes. Cool completely before putting in refrigerator. Chill and serve.

Country Meat Pâté with Walnuts

Pâté de Viandes aux Noix

SERVES 6

10 ounces chicken livers

Salt and freshly ground pepper

4 tablespoons Madeira or port

1 pound sausage meat, chopped

1 pound chopped veal

3 eggs

2 tablespoons fresh chopped fines herbes (use one or as many as you wish
of the following: parsley, chervil, chives, tarragon) or ½ teaspoon
dried thyme

1½ cups walnut halves

1 teaspoon Cognac or other brandy

1. Set aside a glazed ceramic, porcelain, enamelware, or ovenproof glass terrine or other baking dish with a heavy lid.

2. Drain the chicken livers and place them in a shallow bowl. Sprinkle with salt and pepper. Moisten with the Madeira. Let stand 30 minutes.

3. In a bowl, mix the chopped sausage and veal, eggs, fines herbes, and the liquid in which the chicken livers have been soaking. Sprinkle with salt and pepper.

4. Set aside 6 to 12 unbroken walnut halves for decorating the top of the terrine. Coarsely chop the remaining walnuts and set them aside.

5. Preheat oven to 400°. Adjust the rack so that the terrine can be placed in the lower third of the oven. Select a deep baking pan larger than the terrine, and bring water to a boil in the baking pan. (This will be the bain marie into which you will place the terrine.)

6. Cut each chicken liver in half across its thickness.

7. Layer a little more than half the sausage-veal mixture in the bottom of the terrine. Add the halved chicken livers as the second layer. Moisten the chicken livers with drops of Cognac. Sprinkle the chopped walnuts over the livers. Finish with a second layer of sausage-veal hash and decorate the top with the reserved walnut halves.

8. Cover the top with aluminum foil and add the heavy lid. Place the terrine in the bain-marie, checking to make sure the boiling water comes halfway up the side of the terrine. Set the pan in the lower third of the oven and bake for 1 hour and 30 minutes.

9. Chill and serve in slices.

Walnut Quenelles (Dumplings)

Quenelles aux Noix

SERVES 6 (12 DUMPLINGS)

Quenelles (see Note)

1 1/2 cups walnut pieces

1 cup plus 1 tablespoon flour

2 tablespoons walnut oil

3/4 cup water

1/4 teaspoon salt or more, to taste

Freshly ground pepper

5 cups vegetable or chicken stock

Sauce

2 tablespoons butter

1 1/2 tablespoons flour

1/2 cup milk

1/2 cup vegetable or chicken stock

1/4 teaspoon salt or more

3 tablespoons minced parsley, or 3 tablespoons walnuts, coarsely
chopped, for garnish

1. Mince 1 1/2 cups of walnut pieces in the bowl of a food processor or blender,
   to a powder consistency.

2. In a medium bowl, mix 1 cup plus 1 tablespoon flour with the oil, water,
   and powdered walnuts. Season to taste with salt and pepper. Chill the
   paste for at least 2 hours, but no more than 24 hours.

3. To start the sauce with a roux, melt the butter in a medium saucepan over
   low heat. Blend in 1 1/2 tablespoons flour, and continue stirring about 2
   minutes, without browning. Remove the roux from heat. In another pot,

boil the milk and stock together. Pour the boiling liquid into the hot roux, beating quickly with a wire whip to make a smooth sauce. Let the sauce boil, and cook, stirring, for 1 minute. Remove the pan from the heat and add salt to taste.

4. Form the chilled walnut paste into quenelles, or balls about the shape of a walnut. (A good method is to scoop the paste into a wet soup spoon, shape the other side with another wet soup spoon, and then scoop the quenelle out of the first spoon with the second spoon.)

5. Bring stock to a simmer in a large saucepan or deep frying pan. If needed, add enough water so that the poaching liquid is at least 3 inches deep. When stock simmers, add quenelles and cook, with stock gently simmering, for 15 to 20 minutes, or until quenelles puff a little and roll over easily in the stock.

6. Drain the quenelles well. Place on individual plates and nap with the sauce. Garnish with minced nuts or minced parsley.

Note: Quenelle paste should be chilled 2 hours before cooking.

Roquefort-Walnut Quiche

Quiche au Roquefort et aux Noix

SERVES 6

¾ cup walnut pieces

1½ cups (8 ounces) Roquefort cheese

1 cup crème fraîche, or ⅔ cup heavy cream

4 eggs, beaten

4 ounces grated Gruyère cheese

Pinch of freshly ground nutmeg

Single-crust tart dough (see recipe for Pâte Brisée *on page 132)*

Pinch of freshly ground pepper

1. Preheat oven to 400°.

2. In the bowl of a food processor, pulse the walnuts until fine.

3. In a bowl, crumble the Roquefort with a fork. Add the crème fraîche and beaten eggs, and beat with the fork just to mix. Add the grated Gruyère and the chopped walnuts. Stir with the fork to mix lightly.

4. Season the quiche mix with the nutmeg and the pepper. Do not salt, because the Roquefort is salty.

5. Roll out the pastry dough on a lightly floured surface. Lower the dough into the quiche pan and lightly press it into the bottom and sides. Flute the edge of the pastry. Prick the pastry with a fork four or five times. Pour the quiche mixture into the pastry.

6. Cook in the oven for about 40 minutes, or until puffed and beginning to brown on top. Serve immediately.

Stuffed Spanish Mussels

Moules d'Espagne Farcies

SERVES 6

15 walnut halves

2 cloves garlic

16 tablespoons unsalted butter, softened

3 tablespoons minced fresh parsley

Salt and freshly ground pepper

24 large Spanish mussels in their shells, scrubbed and soaked (see Note)

1. Toast the walnut halves using either a toaster oven or a dry hot skillet for just a minute or two, until brown but not burned. Allow to cool. When the walnuts are cool, use a food processor to grind them into a powder.

2. Peel and finely chop the garlic. Place in a bowl. With a fork, mix the garlic, butter, walnut powder, chopped parsley, salt and pepper.

3. Set oven rack and temperature for broiling.

4. Open the mussels by sliding a pointed knife between the two shells. When shells are open, detach the mussel itself from the shell and place it back in the half-shell to which it was attached. Discard the other shell. Arrange the mussel-filled half-shells in a shallow baking dish.

5. Dress each mussel with a portion of the garlic-walnut filling. (The recipe may be prepared ahead of time up to this point. Cover the mussels with a sheet of waxed paper, and refrigerate.)

6. Broil for 2 or 3 minutes, or until the butter bubbles and the filling is lightly browned. Serve immediately.

Note: In France, Spanish mussels would be used for this dish. Elsewhere, use whatever large mussel is available. In the United States, the New Zealand Greenlip mussel is available frozen on the half-shell.

Autumn Quiche with Walnuts

Quiche d'Automne aux Noix

SERVES 6

Single-crust tart dough (see recipe for Pâte Brisée *on page 132)*

1 pound mushrooms of different types, as available (cèpes, girolles, chanterelles, shiitakes, or portobellos)

3 shallots

4 ounces ham, in a chunk or thickly sliced

½ cup dried beans

1 tablespoon walnut oil

1 tablespoon safflower or other mild vegetable oil

4 eggs (2 whole and 2 yolks)

1⅓ cups crème fraîche or 1 cup heavy cream

¼ cup walnut pieces, chopped

Salt and freshly ground pepper

Pinch of freshly ground nutmeg

1. Preheat oven to 400°.

2. On a lightly floured surface, roll out your pastry sheet and place it in a tart pan. Lightly press the pastry into the bottom and sides of the pan. Trim and flute the edge. Prick the pastry several times with a fork. Let stand.

3. Clean the mushrooms, cut off the rough ends, and finely chop. Peel and chop the shallots. Dice the ham coarsely.

4. Cover the pastry with waxed paper and place about ½ cup of dried beans on top, to weight the pastry down. Cook the crust for 10 minutes. Remove from oven and lift off the paper and beans. Lower oven temperature to 350°.

5. Meanwhile, sauté the chopped shallots and diced ham in a mix of the two oils. Add the chopped mushrooms and continue cooking on high heat until the liquid has evaporated. Season with salt and pepper.

6. Beat the whole eggs and yolks together. Mix in the crème fraîche and the chopped walnuts. Add salt and pepper to taste, together with a pinch of nutmeg. Add the mushroom mixture and stir.

7. Pour this preparation into the crust. Bake 35 minutes, or until rounded and golden on top. Serve immediately.

Roquefort-Walnut Omelet

Omelette au Roquefort et aux Noix

SERVES 6

¾ cup walnut pieces

1 cup (5 ounces) crumbled Roquefort cheese

⅔ cup milk

12 eggs

4 tablespoons unsalted butter

Freshly ground pepper

1. In the bowl of a food processor, chop the walnuts until fine. Add Roquefort and milk gradually, while processing continuously to obtain a smooth cream.

2. In a large bowl, beat the eggs with a wire whip only until blended—under a minute. Add the walnut cream and continue to beat just until smooth.

3. Warm the butter in a pan over high heat. When butter simmers and foams, pour the omelet batter into the pan and cook, shaking the pan and smoothing the batter with a fork or spatula. When the bottom is set and the top is still moist, loosen all the edges of the omelet, roll the omelet over once, and turn it onto a serving plate. Sprinkle with pepper to taste.

4. Serve the omelet immediately, accompanied by a green salad.

Rabbit Terrine

Terrine de Lapin

SERVES 6

- 1½ pounds boneless rabbit meat
- ⅔ cup Cognac or other brandy
- ⅔ cup Pineau blanc or other dry white wine
- 2 cloves garlic, chopped
- 5 shallots, chopped
- 2 cups walnut pieces, coarsely chopped
- 2 pounds sausage meat
- Pinch of quatre épices or five-spice powder, allspice, or nutmeg
- Salt and freshly ground pepper
- 2 or 3 bay leaves, fresh if available
- 1 sprig thyme

1. The day before, marinate the rabbit meat in the Cognac and pineau blanc.

2. The next day, drain the rabbit meat, reserving the marinade. Chop the rabbit meat and mix it with the garlic and shallots in a bowl. Add the walnuts, half the marinade, the sausage meat, a pinch of quatre épices, and salt and pepper to taste. Mix, and let stand 1 hour.

3. Set aside an ovenproof terrine or other baking dish with a heavy lid.

4. Preheat oven to 375°. Adjust the rack to the lower third of the oven. Select a deep baking pan larger than the terrine, and bring water to a boil in the pan. (This will be the bain-marie into which you will place the terrine.)

5. Place the meat mix in the terrine and decorate with the bay leaves and thyme. Cover the top with aluminum foil and add the heavy lid. Place the terrine in the bain-marie, with water halfway up the side of the terrine. Set the pan in the lower third of the oven and bake for 2 hours.

6. Allow to cool before refrigerating. Chill and serve in slices.

Chicken Liver Terrine

Terrine de Foies de Volaille

SERVES 6

2 pounds ground pork

1¼ pounds chicken livers, coarsely chopped

4 eggs

¾ cup walnut pieces, coarsely chopped

*6 tablespoons walnut liqueur (liqueur de noix) or other nut liqueur
such as amaretto or crème de noisette*

Salt and freshly ground pepper

2 fresh bay leaves

1 sprig thyme

1. Set aside a glazed ceramic, porcelain, enamelware, or ovenproof glass terrine or other baking dish with a heavy lid.

2. Preheat oven to 300°. Adjust the rack so that the terrine can be placed in the lower third of the oven. Select a deep baking pan larger than the terrine, and bring water to a boil in the baking pan. (This will be the bain marie into which you will place the terrine.)

3. In a large bowl, mix the ground pork, chopped chicken livers, eggs, chopped walnuts, nut liqueur, and salt and pepper to taste.

4. Place the meat mixture in the terrine. Decorate with the bay leaf and thyme. Cover the top with aluminum foil and add the heavy lid. Place the terrine in the bain-marie, checking to make sure the boiling water comes halfway up the side of the terrine. Set the pan in the lower third of the oven and bake for 2 hours.

5. Chill and serve in slices.

Fish

LES POISSONS

Salt Cod Fillets with Walnuts

Crayfish with Walnut Sauce

Mackerel with Walnuts, Rolled in Spinach

Ocean Fish with Walnuts

Salt Cod Fillets with Walnuts

Cod Brandade with Walnuts

Lemon Sole Rolls with Walnuts

Crayfish with Walnut Sauce

Langoustines Sauce aux Noix

SERVES 6

¾ cup walnut pieces

1 clove garlic

¼ cup fresh basil leaves

⅔ cup walnut oil

12 small or 6 serving-size crayfish, or 6 large lobster tails

1. In the bowl of a food processor, finely chop the walnuts. Set aside 3 tablespoons of the chopped walnuts. To the walnuts remaining in the food processor, add garlic, basil, and ⅓ cup of the walnut oil. Mix until smooth.

2. Split each crayfish lengthwise. Over medium flame, heat ⅓ cup walnut oil in a frying pan and sauté all the crayfish for 3 minutes. (For lobster tails, cook 5 minutes.) Season with salt and pepper.

3. Place 1 or 2 crayfish on each plate. Warm the walnut sauce slightly and pour over each crayfish. Sprinkle with the reserved chopped walnuts.

Note: This recipe can be made with lobster tails instead of crayfish. Use 1 lobster tail per person. The sauce is so good that you may be tempted to try it with other seafood, such as sautéed shrimp or broiled swordfish.

Mackerel with Walnuts, Rolled in Spinach

Maquereaux aux Noix en Robe d'Epinards

SERVES 6

1 pound fresh spinach

1 cup walnut pieces, coarsely chopped

3 tablespoons crème fraîche or heavy cream

Salt and freshly ground pepper

6 whole serving-size mackerels (see Note)

2 tablespoons walnut oil

1 steaming tray and pot large enough to hold the fish

1. Remove the roots and tough stems of the spinach. Wash and drain the leaves. Cook no more than 3 minutes in a steamer, just until supple. Carefully remove, spread each leaf out flat on a towel, and allow to drain.

2. In a bowl, mix the chopped walnuts with the crème fraîche. Sprinkle with salt and pepper.

3. Clean the fish by making one long cut along the length of the belly and pulling out the entrails (everything attached to the interior). Cut the heads off. Rinse the fish well with cold water, inside and out, and pat dry. Stuff the interior with the walnut mixture. Close the flap with a toothpick. Brush with walnut oil, then carefully wrap each fish in spinach leaves.

4. Place the fish on a perforated steamer tray over lightly boiling water. Cover, and steam for 25 minutes. Serve immediately.

Note: This recipe can also be made with other small whole fish, such as herring, alewife, shad, perch, or whitefish.

Ocean Fish with Walnuts

Roussette aux Noix

SERVES 6

Court Bouillon

1 onion, peeled

2 whole cloves

2 bay leaves

2 shallots, peeled

1 carrot, quartered

1 sprig thyme

Salt and freshly ground pepper

2½ pounds whole ocean fish such as haddock, mackerel, herring, dog-fish, or ocean perch

1 cup dry white wine

Persillade

2 cloves garlic, peeled and mashed

½ cup chopped fresh parsley

½ cup olive oil

Freshly squeezed juice of 1 lemon

1 sprig thyme

Pinch each of salt and freshly ground black pepper

¾ cup walnut pieces, finely chopped

1. Prepare a court bouillon in a wide, heavy pot by bringing to a boil, in a quart of water, the onion pricked with 2 cloves, the bay leaves, shallots, carrot, thyme, salt, and pepper. Simmer uncovered for 40 minutes.

2. Meanwhile, clean, wash, and dry the whole fish.

3. When the court bouillon is ready, add the white wine and the fish, and simmer on low heat for 10 minutes.

4. Prepare a persillade by mashing the garlic and chopped parsley together. Mix in the oil, juice of the lemon, leaves from a sprig of thyme, salt, and pepper.

5. When the fish are cooked, drain and bone them, leaving the skin and heads on. Arrange the boned fish on a serving platter. Spoon the parsley sauce over the fish and finish with a sprinkling of chopped walnuts. Serve immediately.

Salt Cod Fillets with Walnuts

Filets de Morue aux Noix

SERVES 6

> 2 pounds salt cod fillets
>
> 1 cup walnut pieces, including 12 unbroken halves
>
> ½ cup walnut oil
>
> ⅔ cup safflower oil or other mild vegetable oil

1. Start the desalting process the day before serving. Soak the cod fillets in cold water overnight (or not longer than 24 hours), changing the water several times. Use a glass, stainless steel, or enamel container for this step.

2. Drain the fillets. Place them in a fish poacher (or any wide pot with a lid). Cover with cold water and bring to a simmer. When the water reaches a light simmer and some foam forms, turn the heat off. Cover and let sit for 20 minutes.

3. Meanwhile, set aside 12 attractive walnut halves and finely chop the remaining walnut pieces. Set aside.

4. After the fish have sat for 20 minutes, remove and reserve ½ cup of the cooking water. Drain the fillets. Remove the black and white skin, as well as the bones.

5. Pour the two oils and the reserved ½ cup of cooking water into a stewing pot. Bring this liquid to a boil and add the cod fillets. Lower heat and simmer until the liquid has evaporated. Add the walnut halves, cover, and keep warm without allowing to boil.

6. Arrange cod fillets and walnut halves on a serving platter and sprinkle chopped walnuts down the center of each fillet. Serve accompanied by steamed potatoes.

Cod Brandade with Walnuts

Brandade de Morue aux Noix

SERVES 6

1¼ pounds salt cod fillets

3 or 4 large potatoes

1 bouquet garni (3 sprigs parsley, 1 bay leaf, 1 sprig thyme)

1 cup milk

3 tablespoons walnut oil

Freshly squeezed juice of 1 lemon

2 cloves garlic

1 cup walnut pieces, finely chopped

Freshly ground pepper

½ cup bread crumbs

1 tablespoon unsalted butter

1. Soak the cod fillets in cold water for 6 to 24 hours, changing the water several times. Use a glass, stainless steel, or enamel container for this step.

2. Peel, quarter, and cook the potatoes for 15 minutes in a pot of boiling water.

3. Drain the cod fillets and cut them into large pieces. Bring 8 cups of water and the bouquet garni to a boil in a large pot. Add the cod pieces and poach covered for 3 minutes. Turn the heat off and leave the cod in the pot.

4. Drain and mash the potatoes, adding the milk gradually.

5. Drain the cod. Remove the black and white skin, as well as the bones. Crumble the flesh, gradually adding the walnut oil and lemon juice.

6. Preheat oven to 425°. Peel the garlic cloves and slice into thin slivers.

7. Mix together the mashed potatoes, cod, chopped walnuts, and garlic. Add pepper to taste. Place this mixture in an ovenproof casserole dish. Top with bread crumbs and dot the top with butter. Cook on the top rack of the oven for 15 minutes. Serve hot.

Lemon Sole Rolls with Walnuts

Paupiettes de Limande aux Noix

6 *thin slices bacon*

6 *deboned fillets of lemon sole, without skin (see Note)*

1 *tablespoon chopped chives*

1 *tablespoon chopped chervil*

1 *cup crème fraîche*

Salt and freshly ground pepper

½ *cup unsalted butter*

30 *walnut halves*

1 *tablespoon white wine vinegar*

1. Place the bacon strips in a deep frying pan. Cover with cold water. Bring the water slowly to a boil and simmer uncovered for 5 minutes. Remove from heat and drain.

2. Flatten the sole fillets with a mallet. Be careful not to tear the fillets.

3. Mix the chopped chives and chervil with the crème fraîche. Add salt and pepper to taste.

4. Put a portion of the herbed cream in the center of each flattened fillet. Spread the cream to cover the fillet, stopping ¼ inch from the edges to allow for spreading during rolling. Roll up each fillet.

5. In a nonstick frying pan, cook the blanched bacon on medium heat for about 1 minute on each side. Do not allow the bacon to become crisp. Remove the bacon from the pan. Reserve the drippings in the pan and set aside.

6. Wrap each sole roll in a slice of bacon. Secure each roll with kitchen string. Pour off most of the drippings from the bacon pan, leaving a thin coating on the pan. Add 3 tablespoons of the butter and bring to a sizzle over

medium heat. Cook the sole rolls in the butter, turning carefully to brown on all sides, about 5 minutes in all. Remove each roll to an individual serving plate, leaving the butter in the pan.

7. Sauté the walnut halves in the same pan with the same butter, just until beginning to brown. Remove from pan and allow to drain on paper towels.

8. Add the vinegar and the rest of the butter (5 tablespoons) to the pan, and melt, scraping any cooking bits into the butter. Drizzle this butter over each sole roll. Arrange 5 walnut halves on each plate, surrounding the sole roll. Serve immediately.

Note: This recipe can be made with fillets of any type of sole, flounder, plaice, or dab.

Meat

Duck Breast with Figs Poached in Walnut Wine

Rack of Lamb with Walnut Crust

Duck with Walnut Sauce

Snails with Walnut Sauce

Pork Chops with Walnut Sauce

Turkey Scallops with Morels and Walnuts

Veal Scallops with Walnut Crust

Duck Breast with Blueberry-Walnut Sauce

Veal Rolls with Raisins and Figs

Beef Steak with Roquefort-Walnut Sauce

Partridges Stuffed with Walnuts

Roast Guinea Hen with Apples, Figs, and Prunes

Breast of Veal Stuffed with Walnuts

Honeyed Country Ham

Duck Breast with Figs Poached in Walnut Wine

Canard aux Figues Pochées au Vin de Noix

SERVES 6

3 boned duck breasts (magrets de canard)

12 fresh figs

1¼ cups vin de noix *(see recipe on page 197)*

1 teaspoon chicken stock

3 tablespoons crème fraîche or heavy cream

¾ cup walnut pieces, chopped

1. With a sharp knife, score the skins of the boned duck breasts, without cutting down into the breast meat. Set aside.

2. Wash and remove the stems from the figs. Score the figs lightly, without crushing them. Set aside.

3. Place a heavy frying pan over high heat. Place the scored duck breasts, skin side down, in the hot frying pan. Sauté a few minutes on each side, just until the meat is firm but still pink inside. Remove from heat but keep warm.

4. In a pan with a wide bottom, heat the walnut wine. When it begins to simmer, light it with a match. As the wine flames, add the figs and poach them. Carefully remove the figs from the pan to a bowl you can cover, leaving the poaching liquid in the pan. Cover the figs with a lid or cloth to keep warm.

5. Over medium heat, reduce the poaching liquid. Add the chicken stock and crème fraîche. Cook and allow to thicken for 3 minutes, then add the chopped walnuts.

6. Slice the warm duck breasts, leaving the skin on each piece. On individual warmed plates, arrange slices from half a duck breast, 2 poached figs, and the sauce. Serve immediately.

Rack of Lamb with Walnut Crust

Carré d'Agneau Gratiné aux Noix

SERVES 6

2 racks of lamb, with 6 ribs each

½ cup unsalted butter

Salt and freshly ground pepper

Pinch of cumin

1½ cups walnut pieces

1. Preheat oven to 400°. Position an oven rack in the top third of the oven.

2. Place the racks of lamb in a roasting pan or ovenproof serving dish. Separately melt half the butter and brush the racks on all sides with the butter. Sprinkle with salt, pepper, and cumin.

3. With the meaty side of the lamb facing up, cook in the oven for 20 minutes. Turn the lamb after the first 10 minutes and baste regularly with its juice.

4. Meanwhile, finely chop the walnuts in the bowl of a food processor. Melt the remaining half of the butter in a small frying pan, and cook the walnut powder in the butter very quickly, just to bring out the full flavor of the walnuts and to mix the two ingredients. Remove from heat and set aside. When the racks of lamb have cooked for 20 minutes, remove the pan from the oven and turn the oven temperature to broil. Brush the racks of lamb on all sides with the walnut coating.

5. Place the pan of coated racks of lamb under the broiler very briefly, just long enough to form a stiff crust, but not long enough to burn them. Serve immediately.

Duck with Walnut Sauce

Canard Sauce aux Noix

SERVES 6

1 (5- to 7-pound) duck, cut into serving pieces (see Note)

2 tablespoons oil

2 tablespoons unsalted butter

Salt and freshly ground pepper

4 shallots, minced

¾ cup freshly squeezed orange juice

2 cups chicken stock

Pinch of saffron

Pinch of nutmeg

1 cup crème fraîche, or ¾ cup heavy cream

1 cup walnut pieces, chopped

Rice or pasta to accompany the dish

1. Wash and dry the duck pieces, checking that the pieces are well plucked and flaps of extra fat are removed. (Leave skin on all pieces.) Set aside to dry further.

2. In a heavy casserole with a lid, lightly brown the duck pieces in the oil and 1 tablespoon of the butter. When pieces are golden on all sides, sprinkle with salt and pepper, and remove them from the pan. Add the shallots to the pan and cook them, stirring, until they become translucent. Add the orange juice, chicken stock, saffron, and nutmeg, and stir. Allow to come to a boil. Return duck pieces to the pan, cover, and allow to simmer 1 hour or more, depending on the age and size of the duck.

3. At the end of cooking, remove the duck pieces from the pot, keeping them warm. Strain the cooking liquid through a fine sieve into another heavy casserole and reduce the stock over medium heat for 10 minutes. Add the

crème fraîche, chopped walnuts, and 1 tablespoon of butter. Stir, allowing to reduce for 5 more minutes.

4. Meanwhile, cook rice or pasta and keep warm until serving time.

5. On each plate, place a serving of rice or pasta, with a hollow in the middle. Put a piece of duck in the middle of each mound of rice or pasta and pour the sauce generously over the duck.

Note: This sumptuous recipe works just as well with chicken pieces, but try to buy a stewing or roasting chicken, not a fryer. Whether you use duck or chicken, if you can only find a bird of 4½ pounds or under, it will serve 4, or you can use two birds and serve 8. Don't worry about having leftovers. This dish is marvelous reheated.

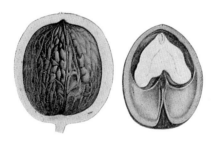

Snails with Walnut Sauce

Casserole de Cagouillesaux Noix

SERVES 6

Court Bouillon

1 cup dry white wine

2 cups water

3 small carrots, peeled and quartered

2 onions, peeled and quartered

2 sprigs parsley

1 bay leaf

1 sprig thyme

¼ teaspoon salt

6 peppercorns

1 cup walnut pieces

6 dozen canned snails (see Note)

4 tablespoons unsalted butter

1 cup crème fraîche, or 3/4 cup heavy cream

1. In a large casserole, make your court bouillon by bringing to a boil the wine, water, carrots, onions, parsley, bay leaf, thyme, salt, and peppercorns, lowering the heat, and simmering for 30 minutes.

2. Meanwhile, chop the walnuts and set aside. Drain the snails.

3. When the court bouillon has simmered 30 minutes, increase heat and bring to a boil again. Add the drained snails. Lower heat and simmer 15 minutes.

4. Remove the snails from the pot and allow them to drain. Strain and reserve the court bouillon.

5. In a casserole, heat the butter until it starts to foam, add the drained snails, and sauté for 2 minutes. Add half of the strained court bouillon and simmer rapidly to reduce by half.

6. Add crème fraîche, continuing to stir and simmer rapidly to reduce, until the sauce is smooth and thick. Reduce the heat, add the chopped walnuts, and stir just to warm the walnuts. Remove from heat and serve.

Note: Canned snails are available at most specialty foods stores.

Pork Chops with Walnut Sauce

Côtes de Porc aux Noix

SERVES 6

> 4 tablespoons unsalted butter
>
> 6 pork chops, 1 inch thick or less
>
> Salt and freshly ground pepper
>
> Freshly squeezed juice of ½ lemon
>
> 1 cup walnut pieces, coarsely chopped
>
> 1 cup crème fraîche, or 3/4 cup heavy cream

1. In a frying pan, heat the butter to foaming and add the pork chops. Sprinkle with salt and pepper. Cook just until the meat is white or grayish throughout. Remove the chops from the pan and keep them warm.

2. To the same pan, add the lemon juice and chopped walnuts. With heat on, stir with a wooden spoon, scraping up the pan bits and juices and stirring them into the sauce. Add crème fraîche, stirring continuously to thicken. Remove from heat. Add salt and pepper to taste.

3. On each plate, place one chop and coat it with the sauce. Serve immediately.

Turkey Scallops with Morels and Walnuts

Dinde Sautée aux Morilles et Noix

SERVES 6

1 onion

6 slices lean bacon

1 ounce morel mushrooms or other available pungent mushrooms, such as shiitakes, portobellos, or cèpes

1 green bell pepper

2 cloves garlic

1 stalk celery

3 carrots

3 tomatoes

6 slices (scallops) uncooked turkey breast, about 1 pound

1 1/4 cups walnut pieces

4 tablespoons vegetable oil

2 tablespoons unsalted butter

1 cup dry white wine

Salt and freshly ground pepper

Pasta to accompany the dish

1. Peel and finely mince the onion. Place in a small bowl. Dice the bacon. Add to the onions and set aside.

2. Wipe the mushrooms clean with a damp paper towel, cut off stem ends, and slice. Set aside.

3. Remove the seeds and membranes from the green pepper and thinly slice. Peel and chop the garlic. Clean the celery and carrots, and thinly slice,

discarding root ends and tops. Wash, dry, core, and coarsely chop the tomatoes. All these vegetables can go into the same bowl.

4. Cut each turkey scallop into 8 pieces. Reserve. In the bowl of a food processor, finely mince the walnut pieces.

5. Heat 2 tablespoons vegetable oil in a frying pan and sauté the bacon and onion until they begin to crisp. Add the mushrooms and cook 3 minutes. Then add the tomatoes, green pepper, garlic, celery, carrots, tomatoes, and the white wine. Sprinkle with salt and pepper. Bring to a simmer, lower heat, and allow to reduce for 15 minutes.

6. Meanwhile, heat the butter and 2 tablespoons of vegetable oil in another frying pan, and lightly sauté the turkey pieces for a few minutes, only until cooked through. Sprinkle with salt and pepper to taste. Just before turning off the heat, sprinkle all the minced walnuts over the turkey and toss.

7. On each plate, place a mound of pasta with a hollow in the middle. In the hollow, place some of walnut-coated turkey. Pour the mushroom-and-vegetable sauce over each serving. Serve immediately.

Veal Scallops with Walnut Crust

Escalopes de Veau Panées aux Noix

> 1¼ cups walnut pieces
>
> ½ cup bread crumbs
>
> 2 eggs, well beaten
>
> 6 veal scallops (thin cutlets)
>
> Salt and freshly ground pepper
>
> 3 tablespoons vegetable oil
>
> 1 tablespoon butter
>
> 6 sprigs parsley, for garnish

1. In the bowl of a food processor, finely chop or grate walnut pieces. In a shallow dish, combine the resulting walnut powder with the bread crumbs.

2. With a meat mallet or the flat side of a hammer, pound and flatten the veal scallops. Then sprinkle with salt and pepper.

3. Dredge each scallop in the beaten egg until evenly coated. Then dredge the scallop in the walnut and bread crumbs until evenly coated. Set each scallop aside on a piece of waxed paper or a rack.

4. Heat the oil and butter in a large frying pan over medium-high heat. Add breaded scallops. When the scallops start to shrink (about 2 minutes on each side), lower the heat to avoid burning the bread coating. Cook about 6 more minutes on low heat.

5. Present the veal scallops on a serving platter garnished with sprigs of parsley. Serve immediately.

Duck Breast with Blueberry-Walnut Sauce

Magret de Canard Sauce aux Myrtilles et aux Noix

SERVES 6

- ¾ cup walnut halves
- 1 pint blueberries
- 2 oranges
- ½ cup firmly packed light brown sugar
- Pinch of cinnamon
- 2 whole cloves
- ¼ teaspoon freshly grated nutmeg
- 6 small boned duck breast halves, about 2 pounds
- Salt and freshly ground pepper

1. Set aside 6 unbroken walnut halves for the garnish. In the bowl of a food processor, coarsely chop remaining walnuts. Wash blueberries, removing any stems. Wash oranges. Grate the rind of 1 orange. Juice both oranges.

2. In a saucepan over low heat, warm the orange juice, zest, brown sugar, cinnamon, whole cloves, and grated nutmeg. When the brown sugar has melted, add the blueberries. Allow to boil for 10 minutes. Add the chopped walnuts. Stir and reduce for a few minutes. Remove from heat.

3. Meanwhile, heat a heavy frying pan over high heat and cook the duck breasts without any oil, starting with the skin side. As they render fat, pour the extra fat off. Cook until golden on both sides and the meat is firm to the touch but still pink in the middle. Sprinkle with salt and pepper.

4. Slice each breast thinly. Spread a sliced duck breast on each plate, and bathe it with the blueberry sauce. Garnish each plate with a walnut half. Serve immediately. Baked squash makes an excellent accompaniment.

Veal Rolls with Raisins and Figs

Paupiettes de Veau aux Fruits Secs

½ cup raisins, divided into two bowls

6 veal scallops (thin cutlets)

Salt and freshly ground pepper

6 thin slices bacon

6 fresh sage leaves

½ cup walnut pieces, chopped

¼ cup pine nuts

1 scant cup grated Parmesan cheese

2 tablespoons vegetable oil

4 tablespoons unsalted butter

4 medium shallots, peeled

2 cloves garlic, peeled

⅔ cup dry white wine

1¼ cups veal, beef, chicken, or vegetable stock

1 sprig of rosemary leaves (about 2 tablespoons)

6 dried figs

Kitchen twine or toothpicks

1. Soak the raisins in warm water.

2. Flatten the scallops lightly with a mallet or bottom of a heavy pan, then sprinkle with salt and pepper.

3. Evenly layer on each scallop: 1 slice bacon, 1 sage leaf, the chopped walnuts

and pine nuts, half the raisins (¼ cup total), and the Parmesan cheese. Roll each scallop, folding in the ends, and fasten with twine or toothpicks.

4. Over medium-high flame, heat the oil and 2 teaspoons of the butter with the garlic and shallots. Sauté the veal rolls until they begin to brown. Add the white wine, stock, rosemary, the remaining raisins, and the dried figs.

5. Lower heat, cover, and simmer for 30 minutes.

6. When ready to serve, remove veal rolls to a warm plate. Add remaining butter to the sauce in the pan and whisk until smooth over low heat. Pour sauce over veal rolls and serve.

Beef Steak with Roquefort-Walnut Sauce

Pavé de Boeuf Sauce Roquefort et Noix

SERVES 6

Sauce

1 cup walnut pieces

¾ cup (4 ounces) Roquefort cheese, crumbled

6 tablespoons crème fraîche, or 4 tablespoons heavy cream

6 tablespoons unsalted butter

¼ teaspoon freshly grated nutmeg

3 shallots, chopped

½ cup sweet vermouth

Steaks

6 tenderloin, round, or rump steaks, about 5 ounces each

1 tablespoon vegetable oil

Salt and freshly ground pepper

4 tablespoons Armagnac or other brandy (optional)

Pasta to accompany the dish

1. In the bowl of a food processor, chop and blend the walnuts, Roquefort cheese, crème fraîche, 3 tablespoons of the butter, and the nutmeg.

2. In a saucepan, heat the remaining 3 tablespoons butter and cook the chopped shallots in the butter until they start to become translucent. Add the vermouth and cook until the liquid evaporates. Add the contents of the food processor, stir well, and remove from the burner.

3. If your steaks are tenderloins, flatten them slightly with a meat mallet. If the steaks are from the round or rump, pound them heavily and score them lightly.

4. In a large frying pan, heat the oil over high heat and fry the steaks. When they are done to your taste, pour any oil out of the pan and sprinkle the steaks with salt and freshly ground pepper.

5. If desired, flambé the steaks with the heat on under the pan: Warm the brandy in a small pot and light it with a match. Pour the flaming brandy into the hot pan, shaking the pan so that the brandy spreads over all the steaks. Remove the steaks to a warm plate.

6. Add the contents of the saucepan to the frying pan, stir, and bring to a boil for just a few seconds. Add whatever juices have collected in the steak plate. Stir and remove from the heat.

7. On each plate, place a steak and surround it with a portion of the Roquefort sauce. Serve accompanied by fresh pasta.

Partridges Stuffed with Walnuts

Perdreux Farcis aux Noix

SERVES 6

1 cup raisins

6 tablespoons Cognac, other brandy, or sweet vermouth

2 onions

1 carrot

2 cups walnut pieces

6 small partridges, with hearts and livers (see Note)

Salt and freshly ground pepper

6 slices bacon

3 tablespoons unsalted butter

1 tablespoon vegetable oil

3 bay leaves

Several sprigs thyme or ¼ teaspoon dried thyme

½ cup white wine

6 slices whole wheat bread, lightly toasted

1. Soak the raisins in the Cognac for 2 hours, or, if you are in a hurry, put the raisins and Cognac in a small pot, heat it for 5 minutes on low heat, and let it stand another 10 minutes.

2. Peel and quarter the onions. Peel and dice the carrot. Set aside.

3. Coarsely chop the walnuts and the hearts and livers of the birds. Add the raisins and the liquid in which they soaked to the chopped walnuts, hearts, and livers, and mix. Sprinkle with salt and pepper and stir. Stuff the interior of the birds with this mix. Close each bird's cavity and secure by wrapping a slice of bacon around the legs, fixing with a toothpick. Salt and pepper each bird.

4. In a wide-bottomed casserole, heat the butter and oil, and lightly brown the birds on all sides. Then add the minced carrot, quartered onions, bay leaves, thyme, and white wine. Cover and cook on low heat for 30 minutes.

5. Serve a single bird or piece of a larger bird on a slice of whole-wheat toast. If you are using large birds, remember to serve each guest some stuffing.

Note: This recipe also suits quail, squab, guinea hens, or chicken. Judge quantities by the size of the bird—one small bird per person, or 2 to 4 servings per large bird.

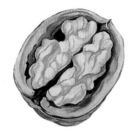

Roast Guinea Hen with Apples, Figs, and Prunes

Pintade aux Pommes, Figues et Pruneaux

SERVES 6

2 small guinea hens, about 2 pounds each (see Note)

1¼ cups walnut pieces

3 tablespoons fromage blanc or heavy cream

¼ teaspoon freshly grated nutmeg

Salt and freshly ground pepper

½ cup chicken stock

1 tablespoon vegetable oil

6 small red apples

6 fresh figs

2 tablespoons unsalted butter

1¼ cups pitted prunes

1. Preheat oven to 425°. Wash the birds, check that their insides are clean and clear, and dry them.

2. In the bowl of a food processor, coarsely chop the walnuts.

3. Place ⅔ of the chopped walnuts in a bowl and mix in the fromage blanc. Add the nutmeg and sprinkle the mixture with salt and pepper. Stir to mix. Stuff the interior of the birds with this nut mixture. Place the birds in a roasting pan large enough to hold them and the fruits. Baste the birds with the chicken stock and vegetable oil. Place the birds in the oven for 15 minutes (or 25 minutes if you are roasting a large chicken).

4. Meanwhile, peel the apples, cut them in half, and core them. Rinse, dry, and quarter the figs. Set aside.

5. Remove the roasting pan from the oven and surround the birds with the apple halves. Dot the apples with small pieces of butter. Return to the oven for 35 minutes (or 45 if you are roasting a large chicken). Baste the birds occasionally with the pan juices.

6. Remove the roasting pan from the oven and add the quartered figs, the prunes, and the rest of the chopped walnuts. Return to the oven for 10 minutes.

7. Serve each guest a portion of bird, fruit, and stuffing.

Note: This delicious recipe also works beautifully with one roasting chicken, or several squabs or Cornish hens. Judge quantities by size. One 3-pound guinea hen serves 3 or 4. A 4- to 5-pound roasting chicken can serve 6. Squabs and Cornish hens are generally small enough that you need one per person.

Stuffed Breast of Veal

Poitrine de Veau Farcie

SERVES 6

1 cup walnut pieces

5 slices bacon

2 tablespoons fresh parsley

¾ cup (4 ounces) crumbled Bleu d'Auvergne or other mild blue cheese

1 egg

Salt and freshly ground pepper

3 pounds boned breast or shoulder of veal

4 tablespoons unsalted butter

1 tablespoon vegetable oil

1 tablespoon fresh thyme leaves or ½ teaspoon dried

1 bay leaf, crushed and broken into pieces

⅔ cup dry white wine

1. Preheat oven to 425°.
2. In the bowl of a food processor, chop the walnuts, bacon, and parsley. Add the Bleu d'Auvergne and egg, and blend. Add a sprinkling of pepper.
3. Hold the veal breast open (or cut a pocket in it) and spread with the stuffing. Roll up the stuffed meat and tie with kitchen twine.
4. Place the stuffed veal in a roasting pan. Rub the veal with the butter and oil. Sprinkle with salt, pepper, thyme leaves, and crushed bay leaf.
5. Cook 1 hour, basting frequently. Add the white wine to the roasting pan and cook another 45 minutes, basting frequently. Remove from the oven.
6. Slice and serve accompanied by a green salad.

Honeyed Country Ham

Palette de Porc au Miel

SERVES 6

1 country ham, such as Virginia, Smithfield, or Kentucky

1 bouquet garni (3 sprigs parsley, 1 bay leaf, and 2 sprigs thyme)

20 peppercorns

Freshly squeezed juice of 1 orange

½ cup acacia honey or other honey

3 tablespoons sherry vinegar

2 teaspoons fresh rosemary leaves or ½ teaspoon dried

8 whole cloves

1¼ cups walnut pieces

18 large pitted prunes

6 fresh figs

1. Soak ham in cold water 24 hours in advance, changing water at least twice.

2. Add bouquet garni and peppercorns, and cover the ham again with cold water in a large pot. Bring to a boil and simmer 1 hour and 30 minutes.

3. Preheat oven to 350°.

4. In a bowl, mix the orange juice, honey, and vinegar. Place the ham in a baking pan. Rub in the rosemary, prick the ham with cloves, and brush with honey mixture. Place in a roasting pan.

5. Cook in the oven for 1 hour. Baste regularly with the cooking juices.

6. Meanwhile, coarsely chop the walnuts and divide them into thirds. Stuff the prunes with two thirds of the chopped walnuts. Wash and quarter the figs.

7. Ten minutes before the end of the cooking, remove the ham from the oven, baste it again with the pan juices, and sprinkle the remaining third of the walnuts over it. Surround the ham with the stuffed prunes and quartered figs. Return to the oven for 10 minutes. Remove and serve hot.

Vegetables and Pastas

LES LÉGUMES ET LES PÂTES

Spaghetti with Walnut Sauce

Spaghetti with Walnut Sauce

Gnocchi with Smoked Ham and Walnuts

Lasagne au Gratin with Wild Mushrooms and Walnuts

Endives au Gratin with Cheese and Walnuts

Eggplant with Roquefort and Walnuts

Spaghetti with Walnut Sauce

Spaghettis Sauce aux Noix

2 teaspoons salt

1 tablespoon vegetable oil

1 pound dried spaghetti

2 cloves garlic, peeled

¾ cup walnut pieces

1¾ cups parsley leaves, firmly packed (see Note)

¼ cup olive oil

Salt and freshly ground pepper

¾ cup grated Parmesan cheese

1 tomato, for garnish (optional)

1. In a large pot, bring approximately 4 quarts of water to a boil and add the 2 teaspoons salt and 1 tablespoon vegetable oil. Add the spaghetti slowly, allowing the water to continue boiling all the time. Cook until noodles are tender, about 10 minutes for dried spaghetti.

2. In the bowl of a food processor, chop and blend the garlic, walnuts, and 1½ cups parsley, reserving ¼ cup of parsley for the garnish. With the motor on, pour the olive oil slowly into the sauce. Sprinkle with salt and pepper and blend again for a moment. Leave sauce in the food processor.

3. Coarsely chop the reserved ¼ cup parsley. If you are using a tomato for garnish, core and dice it. Set aside.

4. Drain the spaghetti, reserving ½ cup of the cooking water.

5. Place a mound of spaghetti on each plate, creating a small indentation in the middle for the sauce. Now check the consistency of the sauce. If it seems too dry, add 1 tablespoon of the cooking water at a time and blend.

The sauce should be dry enough to hold its form as a mound in the middle of the plate, but moist enough to coat the spaghetti when tossed.

6. Place a portion of sauce in the indentation on each mound of spaghetti. Sprinkle each dish with Parmesan cheese, chopped parsley, and diced tomato.

Note: This recipe can be made Italian style by substituting fresh basil for parsley, but parsley is more traditional to southwest France and is a better companion for the walnuts, allowing them to dominate the flavor of the sauce.

Gnocchi with Smoked Ham and Walnuts

Gnocchis au Jambon Fumé et aux Noix

SERVES 6

> 4 ounces smoked ham
>
> ¾ cup walnut pieces
>
> 1 quart milk
>
> 1¼ cups semolina flour (sometimes called pasta flour)
>
> 7 tablespoons unsalted butter, softened
>
> 5 tablespoons grated Parmesan cheese
>
> 2 egg yolks

1. Cut the smoked ham into short strips, about ¼ inch by 1 inch. In the bowl of a food processor, finely chop the walnuts.

2. In a heavy saucepan over medium heat, bring the milk just to a boil. Lower the heat and begin adding the semolina slowly, stirring continuously. Stir over low heat for 10 to 15 minutes, until the semolina thickens in a large mass around the spoon as it turns. Remove the pan from the heat and allow to cool a minute.

3. Beat 4 tablespoons of the butter into the semolina, then 2 tablespoons of the grated Parmesan, and finally the 2 egg yolks. Beat rapidly to avoid coagulating the yolk and to blend the ingredients well.

4. Moisten a marble or other cool surface with drops of cold water. Spread the semolina mixture onto the moist surface, using a metal spatula or the side of a knife to smooth it to a thickness of about ½ inch. Allow to cool for 1 to 3 hours.

5. Preheat oven to 450°. Butter the bottom of a large baking dish.

6. Use a cookie cutter or biscuit cutter to cut the semolina into small disks about 1½ inches in diameter. Set the disks aside onto waxed paper or other nonstick surface. Carefully lift the leftover semolina scraps and line the bottom of the dish with these pieces. Dot with 1 tablespoon of the butter and 1 tablespoon of grated Parmesan.

7. Arrange the semolina disks in one layer, overlapping them. Dot with 2 tablespoons of butter. Sprinkle evenly with the ham strips, chopped walnuts, and the remaining 2 tablespoons grated Parmesan.

8. Bake on the upper rack of the oven for 10 minutes, or until a light crust has formed. Remove from the oven, let cool for a few minutes, and serve.

Lasagne au Gratin with Wild Mushrooms and Walnuts

Lasagnes Gratinées Aux Champignons des Bois et aux Noix

SERVES 6

1 pound various wild mushrooms, such as cèpes, chanterelles, girolles, morels, shiitakes, or portobellos

⅓ cup walnut pieces

2 carrots

1 onion

Fresh chervil, marjoram, or oregano leaves from 1 sprig

Fresh parsley leaves from 1 sprig

7 tablespoons unsalted butter

½ pound ground beef

3/4 cup vin de noix (see recipe on page 197)

Salt and freshly ground pepper

1 pound and 5 ounces fresh lasagne noodles

Béchamel Sauce

1 cup crème fraîche, or 3/4 cup heavy cream

2 cups milk

3 tablespoons flour

1¼ cups (5 ounces) grated French Comté or Gruyère cheese

Salt and freshly ground pepper

1. Clean the mushrooms with a damp paper towel. Mince them and set aside. In the bowl of a food processor, finely chop the walnuts. Leave them in the bowl.

2. Peel the carrots and onion. Add them to the walnuts along with the chervil and parsley, and pulse until finely chopped. Transfer to a heavy casserole dish and sauté over medium heat in 3 tablespoons butter. Add the ground beef and the minced mushrooms, and stir. Add the vin de noix. Sprinkle with salt and pepper. Stir, cover, and allow to simmer for 20 minutes.

3. Meanwhile, prepare the béchamel sauce. In a saucepan, bring the milk to a boil. In a separate heavy saucepan, melt 4 tablespoons butter over low heat. Add 3 tablespoons flour, stirring continuously for 2 minutes. Remove the pan from the heat and add the hot milk gradually, stirring continuously until it is all well blended. Turn the heat on low and stir continuously until the sauce thickens to the consistency of heavy cream. Remove from heat.

4. Add 1 cup of the grated Comté cheese and stir. Sprinkle with salt and pepper. Stir again.

5. Preheat oven to 375°. Butter the bottom of a lasagne pan or rectangular roasting pan.

6. Line the bottom of the pan with a layer of lasagne. Cover with mushroom sauce. Continue with another layer of lasagne topped with béchamel sauce. Repeat this alternation, finishing with a layer of lasagne topped with crème fraîche and sprinkled with the remaining ¼ cup of grated cheese.

7. Bake in the oven for 30 minutes, or until sauce is bubbling and top has formed a crust.

Endives au Gratin with Cheese and Walnuts

Gratin d'Endives Aux Fromages et Noix

SERVES 6

> 1 cup walnut pieces
>
> 3 pounds Belgian or French endive
>
> 1⅓ cups milk
>
> 4 tablespoons butter
>
> ⅓ cup flour
>
> ½ cup (2 ounces) grated Gruyère cheese
>
> ¼ cup (scant 2 ounces) Roquefort or Bleu d'Auvergne cheese
>
> Pinch of nutmeg
>
> Pinch each of salt and freshly ground pepper

1. Preheat oven to 450°. Butter an ovenproof casserole. In the bowl of a food processor, coarsely chop the walnut pieces.

2. Wash the endive and remove the hearts with a pointed knife.

3. Steam the endive for 15 to 20 minutes, until they are tender but not wilting.

4. Remove the endive from the steamer and drain on a towel.

5. Meanwhile, prepare the sauce. In one saucepan, bring the milk to a boil. In another heavy saucepan, melt the butter, add the flour, and stir. When the mixture is smooth, add the hot milk. Cook over low heat for 5 minutes, stirring with a wooden spoon. Remove from the heat and add all but 3 tablespoons of the grated Gruyère, all of the Roquefort or Bleu d'Auvergne, chopped walnuts, nutmeg, salt, and pepper. Stir well.

6. Place the drained endive in the buttered casserole dish. Cover with the sauce. Dot with butter and sprinkle with the reserved grated Gruyère.

7. Bake in the oven for 10 to 15 minutes until a crust forms. Serve hot.

Eggplant with Roquefort and Walnuts

Aubergines au Roquefort et aux Noix

SERVES 6

3 medium eggplants

1 cup walnut pieces

1 cup (5 ounces) Roquefort cheese, crumbled

1 tablespoon tomato paste

1 clove garlic, peeled

Salt and freshly ground pepper

4 tablespoons vegetable oil

½ cup water

1. Preheat oven to 450°.

2. Wash the eggplants and cut them in half lengthwise. Then cut them into 1/4-inch slices lengthwise, without peeling.

3. In the bowl of a food processor, pulse the walnuts to a fine powder. Add the Roquefort, tomato paste, garlic, and a pinch each of salt and pepper. Blend.

4. Coat the bottom of a large baking dish with half the oil. Place a first layer of eggplant slices with skin sides down. Spread with a layer of the Roquefort sauce and continue alternating eggplant and sauce layers with eggplant as the last layer, skin side up.

5. Finish by dripping the rest of the oil and ½ cup of water over the entire dish. Sprinkle with salt and pepper.

6. Cover the dish with aluminum foil. Bake for 10 minutes. Lower the heat to 350° and continue cooking 1 hour and 10 minutes.

7. Serve as an accompaniment to grilled lamb chops or pork chops.

Desserts

LES DESSERTS

Walnut Crêpes

Walnut Charlotte

Caramel-Walnut Custard

White Cheese with Prunes and Walnuts

Walnut Crêpes

Walnut Cream

Walnut Soufflé

Pineapple-Walnut Crêpes

Apple-Walnut Crêpes

Honey-Walnut Crêpe Soufflé

Salad of Dried Fruits

Apricots and Walnuts au Gratin

Pears Stuffed with Walnuts and Raisins

Pears Stuffed with Roquefort and Walnuts

Baked Apples Stuffed with Walnuts

Salad of Wine-Marinated Figs, Prunes, and Raisins

Walnut Charlotte

Charlotte aux Noix

SERVES 6

The charlotte requires 12 hours of chilling before serving. With a very cold refrigerator, 6 hours might do, but the butter in the filling must chill completely in order to ensure a clean unmolding.

1 cup milk

2 egg yolks

1¼ cups sugar

1 cup walnut pieces

1 cup unsalted butter, softened

4 tablespoons walnut eau de vie (see Note)

8 ounces (about 32) small ladyfingers

4 ounces semisweet baking chocolate

1. Bring milk to a simmer in a saucepan. Remove from heat. In a heavy saucepan, beat the egg yolks with ¼ cup of the sugar for about 3 minutes, until the mixture lightens in color. Very slowly add the hot milk in a thin stream, beating continuously. Cook over medium-low heat, stirring continuously, without allowing the custard to approach a simmer. When custard thickens enough to coat the spoon lightly, remove from the heat. Continue beating for a minute to cool the custard. Let stand.

2. In the bowl of a food processor, finely chop the walnuts.

3. In a large mixing bowl, beat 13 tablespoons of the softened butter and gradually add ¾ cups sugar, beating continuously until smooth. Add the chopped walnuts and mix thoroughly.

4. Mix the eau de vie with 4 tablespoons water and ¼ cup sugar. Quickly moisten the ladyfingers with this liquid, without soaking them through.

Line the bottom of a mold (or a springform pan or wide bowl) with the ladyfingers, curved side down. Set aside the remaining ladyfingers.

5. Add the custard to the bowl of walnut-butter mixture and stir until mixed. Pour half the resulting custard-walnut cream into the mold. Cover with a layer of ladyfingers and another layer of the remaining custard walnut cream. Top with the remaining ladyfingers.

6. Chill in the refrigerator for at least 12 hours.

7. When close to serving time, melt the chocolate in a double boiler with 3 tablespoons of butter and 2 tablespoons of water, stirring until smooth. Unmold the charlotte and spoon the chocolate sauce over it.

Note: You may substitute another nut brandy, such as amaretto or crème de noisette, or a plain brandy in which you have warmed several walnuts.

Caramel-Walnut Custard

Crème Brûlée aux Noix

SERVES 6

> 3 *vanilla beans*
>
> 1¼ *cups walnut halves*
>
> 9 *eggs*
>
> 1⅓ *cups sugar, divided into portions of 1 cup and* ⅓ *cup*
>
> 1/2 *cup* vin de noix *(see recipe on page 197)*
>
> 1 *tablespoon unsalted butter*

1. Halve the vanilla beans lengthwise and scrape the interiors with a knife. Set aside the seeds. (The seed casing can be used to flavor sugar or milk for other recipes.)

2. Set aside 6 of the best walnut halves for garnish and finely chop the remaining walnuts.

3. Separate the eggs, placing whites in a large bowl and yolks in another large bowl. Beat the yolks with ⅓ cup of sugar. With a clean dry wire whip or mixer blades, whip the whites until stiff but not dry.

4. Fold the whites into the yolk mixture, carefully turning from the outside toward the inside of the bowl until almost even in color. Fold in the vin de noix, the vanilla seeds, and the chopped walnuts. Pour this mixture into an ovenproof casserole dish or 6 ovenproof custard cups.

5. Bring 1 cup sugar and 4 tablespoons water to a boil in a heavy saucepan. Stir and occasionally shake and swirl the pan to distribute heat evenly. When the mixture turns caramel brown (2 to 3 minutes), add the butter. Stir and add another teaspoon of water. Remove from the heat and beat with a wire whip.

6. Soak the 6 walnut halves in the caramel. Remove and drain.

7. Place a caramelized walnut half on the center of each filled custard cup or in a decorative pattern on the top of the filled casserole dish. Gently pour liquid caramel to coat the top of the custard. Place custard cups or casserole under a hot broiler for 3 or 4 minutes, or long enough to produce a golden, crusty surface. Turn the cups or dish as needed to avoid burning any one area. Serve while still warm.

White Cheese with Prunes and Walnuts

Fromage Blanc aux Pruneaux et aux Noix

SERVES 6

20 pitted prunes

2 cups fromage blanc or plain yogurt

¼ cup crème fraîche or heavy cream

1 cup walnut pieces

Up to 6 tablespoons sugar (optional)

1. Soak the prunes in a bowl of warm water for 1 hour.

2. Meanwhile, beat the fromage blanc with the crème fraîche to produce a light cream.

3. In the bowl of a food processor, finely chop the walnuts. Add the prunes to the processor bowl and purée until smooth. Taste, and add sugar only if necessary.

4. Serve the purée and the cream separately, or blend them.

Walnut Crêpes

Crêpes aux Noix

SERVES 6

Crêpe Batter

2 cups flour

½ teaspoon salt

1½ tablespoons confectioners' sugar

5 eggs

3 cups milk

2 teaspoons unsalted butter, melted

½ cup vegetable oil

Filling

1 cup walnut pieces

¼ cup crème fraîche (or heavy cream)

¾ cup chocolate sauce or puréed apricots, peaches, or pears

1. Prepare the crêpe batter: Sift and then measure the flour. Resift, with the salt and confectioners' sugar, into a mixing bowl. Add eggs and 1½ cups of the milk, the melted butter, and all but 2 teaspoons of the oil. Beat with a wire whip just until the batter is smooth. If the batter seems too thick, stir in a little water. Let stand 1 hour.

2. In the bowl of a food processor, finely chop the walnuts and mix all but 2 tablespoons with the sugar and crème fraîche. Reserve the 2 tablespoons walnuts for the garnish.

3. Grease a crêpe pan with a few drops of the remaining oil. Heat the pan over medium-high heat and quickly pour ¼ cup of batter into the middle of the pan. Tilt the pan back and forth quickly, to cover it with a thin layer of batter. Return to the heat and cook 1 minute. Shake the pan to loosen the crêpe. Lift the crêpe with a spatula, checking that it is lightly browned

and ready for turning. Flip the crêpe over and brown lightly for about 30 seconds. Slide the crêpe onto a plate. Brush the skillet with oil again, and repeat until all the batter is used.

4. Spread the walnut cream in the middle of each crêpe and fold the crêpe over twice, to make a triangle.

5. Serve filled and folded crêpes garnished with a light sprinkling of the remaining chopped walnuts and a few tablespoons of chocolate sauce or puréed apricots, peaches, or pears.

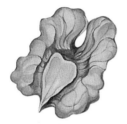

Walnut Cream

Crème aux Noix

SERVES 6

> 1 cup cold milk
>
> 1 egg yolk
>
> ½ cup sugar
>
> 1 tablespoon flour
>
> 2 teaspoons cornstarch
>
> 1 cup walnut pieces
>
> 1 cup crème fraîche, or 3/4 cup heavy cream

1. Begin making a pastry cream by bringing ¾ cup of the milk just to a simmer. Meanwhile, in a second saucepan, beat the egg yolk and sugar, add the flour and cornstarch, then the cold ¼ cup milk, beating until smooth. When the milk has just reached a simmer, remove it from the heat and add it gradually to the mixture in the other saucepan, stirring continuously.

2. Over medium heat, bring this pastry cream to a simmer, stirring vigorously. Cook, stirring, about 20 seconds. Remove from the heat and allow to cool.

3. Meanwhile, in a food processor, finely chop the walnut pieces. In a mixing bowl, whip the crème fraîche until it increases in volume, like whipped cream.

4. Stir the pastry cream occasionally, to help release steam. When it is thoroughly cool, add the whipped crème fraîche to the pastry cream and stir to blend. Add the finely chopped walnuts and mix well.

5. Serve chilled, with cookies.

Walnut Soufflé

Soufflé aux Noix

SERVES 6

1 tablespoon unsalted butter

2 tablespoons confectioners' sugar

1 cup walnut pieces

3 eggs

3 cups milk

⅓ cup sugar

½ cup plain uncooked couscous

1. Preheat oven to 350°. Grease the inside of a soufflé dish and dust with confectioners' sugar.

2. In the bowl of a food processor, finely chop the walnuts. Separate the eggs, putting the yolks in a small bowl and the whites in a large one. Beat the yolks briefly with a fork.

3. In a saucepan, bring the milk and sugar to a boil. Pour the couscous slowly into the milk, stirring just a few times. Allow the mixture to continue cooking until it thickens. Remove from heat. Stir in the chopped walnuts and egg yolks. Allow mixture to cool, stirring occasionally to release steam.

4. Beat the egg whites with a wire whip or electric mixer until they form stiff peaks. Gently fold the beaten egg whites into the warm couscous mixture. Pour the combined mixture into the soufflé dish.

5. Put the soufflé dish in a wide baking pan, adding hot water so that it comes up the side of the soufflé dish about 2 inches. Bake until the soufflé has risen well, about 30 minutes. The time will differ according to the size of the soufflé dish.

Pineapple-Walnut Crêpes

Crêpes à l'Ananas et aux Noix

SERVES 6

Crêpe Batter

¾ cup flour

Pinch of salt

1 teaspoon confectioners' sugar

2 eggs

1¼ cups milk

1 teaspoon orange liqueur

Filling

1 ripe pineapple

1 cup walnut pieces

1 teaspoon pure vanilla extract

1 teaspoon unsalted butter

¼ cup vegetable oil

2 cups crème fraîche, or use vanilla yogurt and omit honey

1 tablespoon honey

1. Prepare the crêpe batter: Sift the flour, salt, and confectioners' sugar into a large bowl. Add the eggs and half the milk. Beat with a wire whip until the batter is smooth. Add the remaining milk and the orange liqueur. Mix and let stand for 1 hour.

2. Meanwhile, prepare the filling: Peel the pineapple, and cut it in half, cross-wise. Dice one half of the pineapple into ¼-inch pieces, discarding any thready pieces. Juice the other half of the pineapple and set the juice aside. In the bowl of a food processor, coarsely chop the walnuts. In a bowl, mix the diced pineapple, half the chopped walnuts, and the vanilla.

3. Preheat oven to 400°. Butter a shallow baking dish.

4. Now make the crêpes: Melt the butter and add it to the batter along with the oil, stirring gently. Grease a crêpe pan with a few drops of oil. Heat the pan over medium-high heat and quickly pour ¼ cup of batter into the middle of the pan. Tilt the pan back and forth quickly, to cover it with a thin layer of batter. Return to the heat and cook 1 minute. Shake the pan to loosen the crêpe. Lift the crêpe with a spatula, checking that it is lightly browned and ready for turning. Flip the crêpe over and brown lightly for about 30 seconds. Slide the crêpe onto a plate. Brush the skillet with oil again, and repeat until all the batter is used.

5. Spread the pineapple filling in the center of each crêpe and roll it up. Place the rolled crêpes in the buttered dish.

6. Combine the crème fraîche, the honey, and 2 tablespoons of the pineapple juice and mix well. Spoon this cream over the rolled crêpes. Sprinkle with the remaining chopped walnuts and bake about 5 minutes, or until the top develops a little crustiness. Serve warm.

Apple-Walnut Crêpes

Crêpes aux Pommes et aux Noix

SERVES 6

Crêpe Batter

1¼ cups flour

½ teaspoon salt

1½ tablespoons sugar

5 eggs

3 cups milk

2 teaspoons unsalted butter, melted

⅓ cup vegetable oil

Filling

4 apples

4 tablespoons unsalted butter

¾ cup confectioners' sugar

1 tablespoon crème fraîche or heavy cream

¼ cup Calvados or other apple brandy

1 cup walnut pieces, coarsely chopped

1. Prepare the crêpe batter: Sift the flour, salt, and 1½ tablespoons sugar into a large bowl. Add eggs and half the milk. Beat with a wire whip until the batter is smooth. Add the remaining milk, the melted butter, and the oil, beating continually with the whip until smooth. If the batter seems too thick, add a little water. Let stand for 1 hour.

2. Meanwhile, prepare the filling: Peel, core, and quarter the apples. Dice them into ¼-inch pieces and sauté in 4 tablespoons butter in a small frying pan over medium heat. When the apples soften, add the confectioners' sugar, crème fraîche, and Calvados. Stir well and continue to cook for a few more minutes. Remove from the heat.

3. Grease a crêpe pan with a few drops of oil. Heat the pan over medium-high heat, and quickly pour ¼ cup of batter into the middle of the pan. Tilt the pan back and forth quickly, to cover it with a thin layer of batter. Return to the heat and cook 1 minute. Shake the pan to loosen the crêpe. Lift the crêpe with a spatula, checking that it is lightly browned and ready for turning. Flip the crêpe over and brown lightly for about 30 seconds. Slide the crêpe onto a plate. Brush the skillet with oil again, and repeat until all the batter is used.

4. Spread the middle of each crêpe with apple filling and sprinkle with chopped walnuts. Roll up each crêpe and serve very warm.

Honey-Walnut Crêpe Soufflé

Crêpes Soufflées au Miel et aux Noix

SERVES 6

Batter

2 cups flour

½ teaspoon salt

1½ tablespoons confectioners' sugar

5 whole eggs

3 egg whites

3 cups milk

2 teaspoons unsalted butter, melted

⅓ cup vegetable oil

Filling

¼ cup sugar

¼ cup honey

¾ cup walnut pieces

2 tablespoons Cognac or other brandy

1. Prepare the crêpe batter: Sift the flour, salt, and confectioners' sugar into a large bowl. Add the 5 whole eggs and half the milk. Beat with a wire whip until the batter is smooth. Add the remaining milk, the melted butter, and the oil, beating continuously until smooth. If the batter seems too thick, mix in a little water. Let stand for 1 hour.

2. Meanwhile, prepare the soufflé filling: In a small saucepan, bring the sugar, honey, and ¼ cup water to a boil, stirring continuously. Remove from heat and cover. In a large bowl, beat the 3 egg whites until they form stiff peaks. Slowly drip the warm syrup into the egg whites, beating continuously, until the mixture cools.

3. Preheat oven to 400°. Butter a rectangular baking dish. In the bowl of a food processor, coarsely chop the walnuts.

4. Grease a crêpe pan with a few drops of oil. Heat the pan over medium-high heat and quickly pour ¼ cup of batter into the middle of the pan. Tilt the pan back and forth quickly, to cover it with a thin layer of batter. Return to the heat and cook 1 minute. Shake the pan to loosen the crêpe. Lift the crêpe with a spatula, checking that it is lightly browned and ready for turning. Flip the crêpe over and brown lightly for about 30 seconds. Slide the crêpe onto a plate. Brush the skillet with oil again, and repeat until all the batter is used.

5. Spoon the soufflé filling into half of each crêpe, garnish with chopped walnuts, and fold in half over the filling.

6. Arrange the folded crêpes in the buttered baking dish and bake for 5 minutes. Remove from the oven, flame the dish with Cognac, and serve warm.

Salad of Dried Fruits

Fruits Secs en Salade

SERVES 6

¼ cup pitted prunes

¼ cup raisins

½ cup Cognac or other brandy

¼ cup dried apricots

¼ cup dried figs

2 oranges

3 Granny Smith apples or other tart apple

¾ cup walnut pieces, coarsely chopped

2 cups mixed hazelnuts, peanuts, and almonds

Freshly squeezed juice of 1 lemon

¼ cup sugar

6 or more fresh mint leaves, for garnish

1. The night before serving, soak the pitted prunes and raisins in the Cognac. Separately soak the dried apricots and figs in a bowl of water.

2. The next day, peel the oranges, taking care to remove all the white membrane. Cut oranges in sections, removing any seeds. Wash, peel, core, and dice the apples.

3. Drain the figs and apricots and cut them in thick slivers.

4. In a large serving bowl, mix the prunes and raisins with the Cognac, slivered apricots and figs, orange slices, diced apples, and chopped walnuts. Add the hazelnuts, peanuts, and almonds. Moisten with the lemon juice and add the sugar. Stir and let marinate in the refrigerator for 4 hours.

5. Serve chilled, garnished with fresh mint leaves.

Apricots and Walnuts au Gratin

Gratinée d'Abricots aux Noix

SERVES 6

1½ pounds fresh apricots or 1 (16-ounce) can apricot halves

¾ cup walnut pieces, coarsely chopped

2 tablespoons cornstarch

2 cups milk

1 vanilla bean, sliced open lengthwise

6 egg yolks

1¾ cups sugar, or 1 ¼ cups if using canned apricots

½ cup rum

1. If you are using fresh apricots, halve them, remove the pits, and cook the fruit over low heat with ½ cup of the sugar and ¾ cup water, for 5 minutes. Remove from heat and drain. (If you are using canned apricot halves, drain them well before using them in step 5.)

2. Prepare the custard: In a small bowl, mix the cornstarch with 3 tablespoons of the milk. In a saucepan, bring the remaining milk to a simmer with the vanilla bean. Remove from heat. Whip the egg yolks with ¾ cup of the sugar. Remove the vanilla bean from the hot milk and pour the milk slowly into the egg yolk mixture, stirring rapidly to release steam. Return this mixture to the saucepan and bring it back to a simmer. Stir and simmer for 1 minute. Remove from heat.

3. Preheat the broiler.

4. Pour the custard into an ovenproof round bowl. Decorate the top of the custard with apricot halves. Sprinkle with chopped walnuts.

5. Heat the rum with the remaining ½ cup sugar and ¼ cup water until sugar is dissolved. Sprinkle this rum sauce over the apricots and custard.

6. Place the dish under the hot broiler for 2 minutes, without allowing the top of the dish to burn, and serve.

Pears Stuffed with Walnuts and Raisins

Poires Farcies

SERVES 6

> 6 *large ripe but firm pears*
>
> ¾ *cup walnut pieces, coarsely chopped*
>
> ¼ *cup raisins*
>
> ¼ *cup honey*
>
> *Freshly squeezed juice of 1 lemon*

1. Preheat oven to 350°.

2. Peel the pears without removing the stem. Cut off the top (stem side) third of each pear. Carefully use a spoon to core and seed both parts of each pear.

3. Mix together the walnuts with the raisins and honey.

4. Stuff the bottom part of each pear with the walnut-raisin mixture. Cover each with its top to reconstruct the pear.

5. Place the pears stem up in an ovenproof dish and pour water into the dish up to the midpoint of the pears. Sprinkle with the lemon juice.

6. Bake 20 minutes, or until the pears are tender when pricked with the point of a knife.

7. Remove the hot pears to a serving platter, leaving the cooking liquid in the dish. Over medium heat, simmer and reduce the liquid and then baste the pears with it. Serve warm.

Pears Stuffed with Roquefort and Walnuts

Poires Farcies au Roquefort et aux Noix

SERVES 6

3 large pears

Freshly squeezed juice of 1 lemon

⅓ cup walnut pieces

4 tablespoons Cognac or other brandy

1 cup (5 ounces) Roquefort cheese

6 tablespoons crème fraîche or plain yogurt

Salt and freshly ground pepper

1. Wipe the pears clean, but do not peel them. Halve them lengthwise.

2. With a spoon, core the pears and make a hollow for the stuffing. Sprinkle the interior with the lemon juice to avoid darkening.

3. Prepare the stuffing: In the bowl of a food processor, finely chop the walnuts. Add the Cognac, Roquefort, crème fraîche, and a sprinkle of salt and pepper. Blend.

4. Serve each pear half with a dollop of stuffing in its hollow. Serve cold.

Baked Apples Stuffed with Walnuts

Pommes Chaudes Farcies aux Noix

SERVES 6

> 1 cup walnut halves
>
> 6 tablespoons unsalted butter, softened
>
> 1/3 cup sugar
>
> 1/4 teaspoon ground cinnamon
>
> 6 apples
>
> 1 cup crème fraîche or vanilla yogurt (optional)

1. Preheat oven to 400°. Grease a baking pan.

2. Set aside 6 of the best walnut halves. In the bowl of a food processor, finely chop the remaining walnuts. Add the softened butter, sugar, and cinnamon. Blend.

3. Peel the apples and remove the cores, starting from the top (stem end) and leaving 1/2 inch of the bottom of the apple intact.

4. Stuff the apples with the walnut mixture. Bake for 20 minutes in the greased baking pan.

5. Serve the apples warm, garnished with the reserved walnut halves. If you wish, accompany the baked apples with a spoonful of whipped crème fraîche.

Salad of Wine-Marinated Figs, Prunes, and Raisins

Salade de Fruits au Vin

SERVES 6

- ¾ *pound fresh figs*
- *1 cup pitted prunes*
- *1 cup red wine*
- *⅔ cup port*
- *¼ cup raisins*
- *⅓ cup rum*
- *Freshly squeezed juice of 1 orange*
- *3 tablespoons honey*
- *Pinch of ground cinnamon*
- *2 cups walnut pieces, coarsely chopped, for garnish*
- *2 tablespoons slivered almonds, for garnish*

1. Wipe the figs clean and quarter them. Put them in a bowl and add the prunes, wine, and port. Put the raisins in a bowl and cover with the rum and warm water to cover. Allow both bowls of fruit to marinate 6 hours or more.

2. Mix together the orange juice and honey and set aside.

3. When the figs, prunes, and raisins have marinated enough, drain them, reserving ¼ cup of the liquid. Add the reserved liquid to the orange juice–honey mixture and stir. Baste the fruit in the bowls with the orange juice–honey mixture and sprinkle with cinnamon. Garnish with the chopped walnuts and slivered almonds and serve.

Tarts

LES TARTES

Walnut Tart

Tart Dough

Sweet Tart Dough

Orange-Chocolate Tart with Walnuts

Banana-Walnut Tart

Walnut Tart

Peach Tart with Walnuts

Pear Tart with Walnuts

Apple Tart with Walnuts

Caramel-Walnut Tart

Tart Dough

Pâte Brisée

SINGLE CRUST FOR A 10-INCH TART

1½ cups sifted flour

8 tablespoons unsalted butter, chilled

½ teaspoon salt

Pinch sugar

½ cup ice water

1. Place the flour in a mixing bowl. Working quickly, quarter the chilled stick of butter lengthwise, and then slice it crosswise in ¼-inch slices. Add the butter pieces to the bowl and use an electric mixer on medium speed to cut the butter into the flour (see Note). Stop as soon as the mixture begins to look like coarse meal. (Little pieces of butter will still be visible.)

2. In a small bowl, add the salt and sugar to the cold water and stir to blend. Pour the liquid into the flour and beat at medium speed until the dough can be gathered into a ball.

3. Gather the dough into a ball. Sprinkle a few drops of cold water on any dough pieces that do not stick together and press them into the ball. Wrap the ball in waxed paper or plastic wrap and refrigerate for 2 hours. (It will store well for 3 days in the refrigerator.)

Note: Directions are given for using an electric mixer, but the dough can be made with excellent results using a food processor. Keep the handling of the dough to a minimum. Use the briefest time possible for each cutting or mixing step.

Sweet Tart Dough

Pâte Sablée

SINGLE CRUST FOR A 10-INCH TART

1¼ cups sifted flour

4 tablespoons sugar

Pinch of baking powder

Pinch of salt

12 tablespoons unsalted butter, chilled

1 egg

½ teaspoon pure vanilla extract

1. Place the flour, sugar, baking powder, and salt in a mixing bowl, and stir with a fork to mix well. Working quickly, quarter the chilled stick of butter lengthwise, and then slice it crosswise in ¼-inch slices. Add the butter pieces to the bowl and use an electric mixer on medium speed to cut the butter into the flour (see Note). Stop as soon as the mixture begins to look like coarse meal. (Little pieces of butter will still be visible.)

2. In a small bowl, mix the egg and vanilla with a fork and pour them over the dough mixture. Beat at medium speed until the dough can be gathered into a ball.

3. Gather the dough into a ball. Sprinkle a few drops of cold water on any dough pieces that do not stick together and press them into the ball. Wrap the ball in waxed paper or plastic wrap and refrigerate for 2 hours. (It will store well for 3 days in the refrigerator.)

Note: Directions are given for using an electric mixer, but the dough can be made with excellent results using a food processor. Keep the handling of the dough to a minimum. Use the briefest time possible for each cutting or mixing step.

Orange-Chocolate Tart with Walnuts

Tarte au Chocolat à l'Orange et aux Noix

SERVES 6 TO 8

Single-crust tart dough (see recipe for Pâte Brisée *on page 132)*

7 ounces unsweetened chocolate

¾ cup walnut halves

3 eggs

¾ cup sugar

⅔ cup crème fraîche, or ½ cup heavy cream

½ cup milk

1 orange

2 tablespoons confectioners' sugar

1. Preheat oven to 375°. Use a 10-inch tart pan, preferably one with a removable bottom.

2. Roll out the dough on a lightly floured surface and place it in the tart pan, pinching or fluting the edge. Prick the crust with a fork in several places. Cover the crust with waxed paper and weight paper down with dried beans. Bake for 10 minutes. Remove from oven. Carefully remove waxed paper and beans, and let crust cool. Lower oven to 325°.

3. Melt the chocolate in a double boiler, and set aside. Set aside 8 unbroken walnut halves and, in the bowl of a food processor, finely chop the remaining walnuts. Grate the orange rind until you have a teaspoon of zest. Juice the orange and reserve the juice.

4. In a mixing bowl, beat the eggs and sugar until smooth and light in color. Gradually add the melted chocolate, crème fraîche, milk, orange juice, and 1 teaspoon of the orange zest. Beat until smooth. Add the chopped

walnuts and stir to incorporate them evenly. Pour this mixture into the bottom of the precooked crust.

5. Bake 15 minutes. Remove from the oven and allow to cool.

6. Powder the top of the tart with confectioners' sugar, and decorate with the reserved walnut halves. If you used a tart pan with a removable bottom, unmold the tart.

Banana-Walnut Tart

Tarte aux Noix et aux Bananes

SERVES 6 TO 8

Single-crust tart dough (see recipe for **Pâte Brisée** *on page 132)*

4 eggs

1 cup sugar

1 teaspoon pure vanilla extract

¾ cup walnut halves

4 bananas

1 cup crème fraîche, or ¾ cup heavy cream

Freshly squeezed juice of 1 lemon

2 tablespoons confectioners' sugar

1. Preheat oven to 375°. Use a 10-inch tart pan, preferably one with a removable bottom.

2. Roll out the dough on a lightly floured surface and place it in the tart pan, pinching or fluting the edge. Prick the crust with a fork in several places.

3. In a mixing bowl, beat together the eggs, sugar, and vanilla until the mixture is smooth and light in color.

4. Set aside 8 unbroken walnut halves. In the bowl of a food processor, coarsely chop the remaining walnuts. Add the peeled bananas, crème fraîche, and lemon juice. Blend. Pour this blend into the mixing bowl with the egg-sugar mixture. Beat a minute to blend. Pour the batter into the crust.

5. Bake 25 minutes, or until the batter has set. Remove from the oven and allow to cool.

6. Powder the top of the tart with confectioners' sugar and garnish with reserved walnut halves. If you used a tart pan with a removable bottom, unmold the tart.

Walnut Tart

Tarte aux Noix

SERVES 6 TO 8

Single-crust sweet tart dough (see recipe for Pâte Sablée *on page 133)*

1¼ cups walnut halves

2 eggs

½ cup sugar

1 cup crème fraîche, or ¾ cup heavy cream

1 teaspoon ground cinnamon

2 tablespoons confectioners' sugar

1. Preheat oven to 375°. Use a 10-inch tart pan, preferably one with a removable bottom.

2. Roll out your dough on a lightly floured surface and place it in the tart pan, pinching or fluting the edge. Prick the crust with a fork in several places.

3. Set aside 8 unbroken walnut halves and finely chop the remaining walnuts in the bowl of a food processor.

4. In a mixing bowl, beat the eggs with the sugar until smooth and light in color. Add the crème fraîche, cinnamon, and chopped walnuts. Mix well. Pour the walnut mixture into the crust.

5. Bake for 40 minutes. Remove from the oven and allow to cool.

6. Powder the top of the tart with confectioners' sugar and garnish with the reserved walnut halves. If you used a tart pan with a removable bottom, unmold the tart.

Peach Tart with Walnuts

Tarte aux Pêches et aux Noix

SERVES 6 TO 8

Single-crust sweet tart dough (see recipe for Pâte Sablée *on page 133)*

1¼ cups walnut halves

6 tablespoons unsalted butter

⅓ cup sugar

1 teaspoon vanilla extract

1 egg

6 large peaches

1. Preheat oven to 375°. Use a 10-inch tart pan, preferably one with a removable bottom.

2. Roll out your dough on a lightly floured surface and place it in the tart pan, pinching or fluting the edge. Prick the crust with a fork in several places.

3. Set aside the 8 best walnut halves and finely chop the remaining walnuts in the bowl of a food processor. Melt the butter over low heat and remove from heat.

4. In a mixing bowl, beat together the sugar, vanilla, egg, and melted butter until smooth. Add the chopped walnuts, mix well, and pour the mixture into the tart pan. Use a spatula to smooth the mixture evenly in the tart pan.

5. Blanch the peaches for 30 seconds in boiling water to loosen the skin. Peel, halve, and pit the peaches. Thinly slice each peach. Arrange the slices over the walnut mixture in the tart pan, overlapping the slices. Garnish with the reserved walnut halves.

6. Bake for 30 to 35 minutes or until golden on top. Remove from the oven and allow to cool. If you used a tart pan with a removable bottom, unmold the tart.

Pear Tart with Walnuts

Tarte aux Poires et aux Noix

SERVES 6 TO 8

Single-crust tart dough (see recipe for Pâte Brisée *on page 132)*

1 (16-ounce) can pear halves

2 eggs

½ cup sugar

⅔ cup crème fraîche or ½ cup heavy cream

1 teaspoon ground cinnamon

1 teaspoon pure vanilla extract

⅔ cup walnut pieces, minced

1. Preheat oven to 375°. Use a 10-inch tart pan, preferably one with a removable bottom.

2. Roll out your dough on a lightly floured surface and place it in the tart pan, pinching or fluting the edge. Prick the crust with a fork in several places. Cover crust with waxed paper and weight with dried beans. Bake for 10 minutes. Remove waxed paper and beans and let the crust cool.

3. Meanwhile, drain the pears. Cut pear halves into ¼-inch slices (see Note).

4. In a bowl, beat the eggs and sugar until smooth and light yellow. Add the crème fraîche, cinnamon, vanilla, and minced walnuts. Mix thoroughly.

5. Arrange the sliced pears on the bottom of the precooked crust and pour the creamy nut mixture over the pears.

6. Bake for 20 to 30 minutes, until top of tart has begun to lightly brown. Remove from the oven and allow to cool. Unmold the tart.

Note: To produce a classic French tart, layer the pear slices over each other at ½-inch intervals. To produce a heartier tart, hold each pear half intact as you slice it. Then put a spatula under each pear, and place it intact on the pear tart, with the wide end toward the outer rim and the point toward the center.

Apple Tart with Walnuts

Tarte aux Pommes et aux Noix

SERVES 6 TO 8

Single-crust tart dough (see recipe for Pâte Brisée *on page 132)*

3 apples

2 cups walnut halves

⅓ cup honey

½ cup crème fraîche, or ⅓ cup heavy cream

1. Preheat oven to 350°. Use a 10-inch tart pan, preferably one with a removable bottom.

2. Roll out your dough on a lightly floured surface and place it in the tart pan, pinching or fluting the edge. Prick the crust with a fork in several places. Refrigerate the tart pan until ready to fill.

3. Peel, core, and quarter the apples. Dice them into ¼-inch pieces. Place the diced apples in a saucepan with 2 tablespoons of water and cook over medium heat until they reduce to a marmalade.

4. Meanwhile, divide the walnuts into two equal portions, with the more attractive walnut halves all in one portion. In the bowl of a food processor, finely chop the less attractive walnuts. Reserve the other walnut halves.

5. When the apples have softened to marmalade texture, remove the saucepan from the heat. Add half the honey, all the crème fraîche, and the chopped walnuts. Stir to mix.

6. Remove the prepared crust from the refrigerator and pour in the apple marmalade. Garnish with the reserved walnut halves. Thread the remaining honey over the top of the tart.

7. Bake for 40 minutes. Remove from the oven and allow to cool. If you used a tart pan with a removable bottom, unmold the tart.

Caramel-Walnut Tart

Tarte au Caramel et aux Noix

SERVES 6 TO 8

Single-crust sweet tart dough (see recipe for Pâte Sablée on page 133)

3 cups walnut halves

1¼ cups sugar

½ cup water

3 tablespoons walnut liqueur (liqueur de noix, or see Note)

1 cup crème fraîche, or ⅔ cup heavy cream

1. Preheat oven to 375°. Use a 10-inch tart pan, preferably one with a removable bottom.

2. Roll out your dough on a lightly floured surface and place it in the tart pan, pinching or fluting the edge. Prick the crust with a fork in several places. Cover the crust with waxed paper and weight the paper down with dried beans. Bake for 10 minutes. Carefully remove the waxed paper and beans. Return the crust to the oven for 2 to 5 minutes, until lightly browned. Remove from oven and allow to cool.

3. Arrange the walnut halves over the pie crust.

4. Prepare a caramel sauce: In a saucepan, combine the sugar, water, and liqueur, and cook over low heat until the liquid becomes golden. Then add the crème fraîche, stirring continuously for 2 to 3 minutes.

5. Pour the hot caramel sauce over the walnuts in the tart. Allow to cool.

Note: you may also substitute another nut liqueur, such as amaretto or crème de noisette, or a plain brandy in which you have warmed several walnuts.

Cakes

LES GÂTEAUX

Traditional Walnut Cake

Banana-Walnut Cake

Fig and Walnut Cake

Walnut-Prune Cake

Chocolate-Walnut Cake

Yogurt-Walnut Cake

Chilled Walnut Charlotte

Traditional Walnut Cake

Walnut Cake with Spirits

Meringue Cake with Walnut Cream

Bread Crumb Cake with Walnuts

Honey Cake Roll with Walnuts

Mocha-Walnut Cake

Honey-Walnut Cake

Honey-Walnut Spice Cake

Banana-Walnut Cake

Cake aux Bananes et aux Noix

SERVES 6 TO 8

9 tablespoons unsalted butter, softened

⅔ cup sugar

2 eggs, lightly beaten

1½ cups sifted flour

1 teaspoon baking powder

¾ cups walnut pieces

3 ripe bananas

¼ teaspoon ground cinnamon

1. Preheat oven to 350°. Grease and flour sides and bottom of a 9-inch round cake pan.

2. Beat the softened butter with the sugar until creamy. Add the beaten eggs and beat 1 minute. Sift the flour and baking soda into the batter, continuing to beat just until blended.

3. In the bowl of a food processor, coarsely chop the walnuts and add them to the batter. Put the bananas and cinnamon in the same bowl and pulse until well mixed. Add banana-cinnamon mixture to the batter and stir the batter until well blended. Pour the batter into the prepared cake pan.

4. Bake for 50 minutes to 1 hour, or until rounded and golden on top. Let cool for 10 minutes. Loosen the sides by running a knife around the side of the pan. Turn the cake onto a cooling rack with a quick jerk. Immediately reverse the cake and let it cool top-side up.

Fig and Walnut Cake

Cake aux Noix et aux Figues

SERVES 6 TO 8

9 tablespoons unsalted butter, softened

³/4 cup sugar

3 eggs, lightly beaten

1 cup plus 2 tablespoons sifted flour

1 teaspoon baking powder

¹/2 cup strong coffee

1 cup dried figs

1 cup walnut pieces, coarsely chopped

¹/4 cup semisweet chocolate chips

1. Preheat oven to 350°. Grease and flour sides and bottom of a 9-inch round cake pan.

2. In a mixing bowl, beat the softened butter. Add the sugar and continue beating until creamy. Add the eggs and beat another minute. Sift the flour and baking powder into the batter, continuing to beat until smooth. Fold in the strong coffee.

3. Dice the figs. Add figs, walnuts, and chocolate chips to the batter and stir well. Pour the batter into the prepared cake pan.

4. Bake for 45 minutes, or until the cake is well risen and golden. Let cool for 10 minutes. Loosen the sides by running a knife around the side of the pan. Turn the cake onto a cooling rack with a quick jerk. Immediately reverse the cake and let it cool top-side up.

5. Serve alone or with a walnut ice cream (see pages 180–183 for assorted ice cream recipes).

Walnut-Prune Cake

Cake aux Pruneaux et aux Noix

SERVES 6 TO 8

> 9 tablespoons unsalted butter, softened
>
> 1¼ cups sugar
>
> 5 eggs
>
> ⅔ cup finely ground almonds
>
> Scant ⅔ cup sifted flour
>
> ½ teaspoon baking powder
>
> 2 tablespoons Cognac or other brandy
>
> 1 cup pitted prunes
>
> 1 cup walnut pieces, finely chopped

1. Preheat oven to 350°. Grease and flour sides and bottom of a 9-inch round cake pan.

2. In a mixing bowl, beat the softened butter. Add the sugar and beat until creamy. Add the eggs one by one, beating continuously. Add the powdered almonds. Sift the flour and baking powder into the batter, beating until smooth. Finally, fold in the brandy.

3. In the bowl of a food processor, finely chop the walnuts. Dice the pitted prunes into ¼-inch pieces.

4. Add the chopped walnuts and diced prunes to the batter. Pour the batter into the prepared cake pan.

5. Bake for about 45 minutes, or until the top is rounded and golden. Let cool for 10 minutes. Loosen the sides by running a knife around the side of the pan. Turn the cake onto a cooling rack with a quick jerk. Immediately reverse the cake and let it cool top-side up.

6. Serve slices alone or with a small scoop of walnut ice cream (see pages 180–183 for ice cream recipes).

Chocolate-Walnut Cake

Gâteau au Chocolat et aux Noix

SERVES 6

4 ounces semisweet baking chocolate

9 tablespoons unsalted butter, softened

⅔ cup sugar

3 eggs

⅓ cup sifted flour

½ teaspoon baking powder

Pinch of salt

1 cup walnut pieces, coarsely chopped

Confectioners' sugar

1. Preheat oven to 425°. Butter and flour an 8-inch round cake pan.

2. Melt the chocolate in a double-boiler over boiling water.

3. When chocolate is melted, take the top of the double boiler off the boiling water and let the melted chocolate cool while you do the next step.

4. In a mixing bowl, beat the softened butter. Add the sugar and beat until creamy. Add the eggs one by one, beating continuously. Sift the flour, baking powder, and salt into the batter, beating until smooth. Add the melted chocolate and chopped walnuts, and mix well. Pour the batter into the prepared cake pan.

5. Bake for 20 minutes. Let cool for 10 minutes. Loosen the sides by running a knife around the side of the pan. Turn the cake onto a cooling rack with a quick jerk. Immediately reverse the cake onto another cooling rack and let it cool top-side up.

6. Just before serving, sift a few tablespoons of confectioners' sugar evenly over the top of the cake.

Yogurt-Walnut Cake

Gâteau au Yaourt et aux Noix

SERVES 6

2 cups walnut halves

2 eggs

1 cup sugar

1 cup plain yogurt

1 cup sifted flour

½ teaspoon baking powder

1. Preheat oven to 375°. Grease and flour an 8-inch springform pan. (If a springform is not available, use an 8-inch round cake pan.)

2. Set aside 6 unbroken walnut halves and finely chop the remaining walnuts in the bowl of a food processor.

3. In a mixing bowl, blend the eggs with the sugar. Beat well for 2 minutes. Add the yogurt, flour, and baking powder. Beat 1 minute. Then add the chopped walnuts. Beat another minute. Pour the batter into the prepared cake pan.

4. Bake for 35 minutes, or until a knife or cake tester comes out clean. Let cool for 10 minutes. Loosen the sides by running a knife around the side of the pan. If you are using a springform pan, open it and loosen the bottom of the cake with a spatula. Turn the cake onto a cooling rack with a quick jerk. Immediately reverse the cake onto another cooling rack and garnish with the reserved walnut halves. Let the cake cool top-side up.

Chilled Walnut Charlotte

Gâteau aux Noix I

SERVES 6

This cake needs at least 6 to 12 hours of refrigeration (depending on the temperature in your refrigerator).

4 ounces unsweetened baking chocolate

2 cups walnut pieces, finely chopped

1 cup unsalted butter, softened

1¼ cups sugar

2 eggs

24 ladyfingers

1. Use a round cake pan, mold, or casserole, 7 to 8 inches in diameter and 4 inches high. Line the bottom of the pan with a round of aluminum foil.

2. Melt the chocolate in a double boiler over boiling water.

3. Meanwhile, finely chop the walnuts in the bowl of a food processor. When the chocolate is melted, lift the pot off the water and set aside to cool while you do the next step.

4. In a mixing bowl, beat the softened butter. Add the sugar and beat until creamy. Separate the eggs, putting the whites into a bowl large enough for whipping. Add the yolks to the butter-sugar mixture, along with the melted chocolate and chopped walnuts. Mix this batter until smooth.

5. Whip the egg whites until stiff but not dry and fold them gently into the walnut cream until it is almost, but not completely, smooth.

6. Fit the ladyfingers closely, curved side down, in the bottom of the pan. Cover them with one third of the walnut cream. Repeat with alternating layers, finishing with ladyfingers if there are enough left.

7. Chill in the refrigerator for at least 6 hours, or overnight. Unmold just before serving.

Traditional Walnut Cake

Gâteau aux Noix II

SERVES 6

1¼ cups walnut pieces, including 7 unbroken walnut halves

10 tablespoons unsalted butter, softened

¾ cup sugar

3 eggs

1¾ cups sifted flour

1 teaspoon baking powder

Pinch of salt

1. Preheat oven to 350°. Grease and flour a 9-inch springform pan. (Use a 9-inch cake pan if you do not have a springform pan.)

2. Set aside 7 of the best walnut halves and coarsely chop the remaining walnuts in the bowl of a food processor.

3. In a mixing bowl, beat the butter. Add the sugar, eggs, flour, baking powder, and salt one ingredient at a time, beating continuously. When the ingredients are well mixed, add the chopped walnuts and mix evenly. Pour the batter into the prepared pan.

4. Bake for 45 minutes. Let cool for 10 minutes. Loosen the sides by running a knife around the side of the pan. If you are using a springform pan, open it and loosen the bottom of the cake with a spatula. Turn the cake onto a cooling rack with a quick jerk. Immediately reverse the cake onto another cooling rack and garnish with the reserved walnut halves. Let the cake cool top-side up.

Walnut Cake with Spirits

Gâteau aux Noix III

SERVES 6

½ cup butter

1½ cups walnut halves

4 whole eggs and 2 egg whites

⅓ cup sugar

⅓ cup sifted flour

Pinch of salt

1 tablespoon walnut liqueur (liqueur de noix, or see Note)

1 teaspoon pure vanilla extract

Confectioners' sugar

1. Preheat oven to 375°. Grease and flour a 9-inch springform pan. (Use a 9-inch cake pan if you do not have a springform pan.)

2. Melt the butter over low heat and set aside. Meanwhile, set aside 7 good walnut halves and chop remaining walnuts in the bowl of a food processor.

3. In a mixing bowl, either by hand or on a low mixer speed, blend the whole eggs and sugar. Then sift the flour into the bowl and stir or mix until smooth. Add the melted butter, salt, nut liqueur, and vanilla. Stir a few times and add the chopped nuts, stirring until well mixed.

4. In a separate bowl, beat the egg whites until soft peaks form. With a large spoon, gently fold the beaten egg whites into the batter just until blended. Pour the batter into the prepared pan.

5. Bake for 25 minutes, or until a knife or cake tester comes out clean. Allow to cool and then remove the cake from the pan. Dust with confectioners' sugar and garnish with the reserved walnut halves.

Note: You may substitute another nut liqueur, such as amaretto or crème de noisette, or a plain brandy in which several walnuts have been warmed.

Meringue Cake with Walnut Cream

Gâteau Meringué à la Crème de Noix

SERVES 6

> 3 cups walnut pieces, including 6 unbroken walnut halves
>
> 6 eggs, at room temperature
>
> 1⅓ cups sugar
>
> ¼ teaspoon cream of tartar
>
> 2 cups milk
>
> ⅓ cup sifted flour
>
> 1 teaspoon pure vanilla extract
>
> Confectioners' sugar
>
> 1 cup unsalted butter, softened

1. Preheat oven to 325° and adjust racks to accommodate 2 baking sheets. Line the baking sheets with parchment paper, or grease and flour them.

2. Set aside 6 good walnut halves for garnish. In the bowl of a food processor, reduce the rest of the walnuts to a fine powder, using the fine grating blade or using the chopping blade with pulsing turns, stopping before the nuts become sticky and start to clump. Put ⅓ of the powdered nuts in one container and the remaining nuts in another.

3. Separate the eggs, putting 5 whites in a large mixing bowl, discarding 1 white, and putting 6 yolks in a second mixing bowl.

4. With an electric mixer, beat the egg whites until foamy. Add the cream of tartar and beat. Gradually add ⅔ cup of sugar, while continuing to beat until the meringue forms stiff peaks. With a clean, dry spoon, fold in the smaller portion of powdered walnuts until nearly evenly blended.

5. On each prepared baking sheet, form an 8-inch round disk of meringue using a pastry bag or a spoon and spatula. Bake for 35 to 40 minutes, and remove from the oven to cool.

6. Meanwhile, prepare the walnut cream: Bring the milk to a boil and set aside. In a mixing bowl, beat the egg yolks with ⅔ cup sugar. Sift the flour gradually into this mix, beating continuously. Gradually add the scalded milk while beating. Pour this custard into a saucepan and cook several minutes over medium heat, stirring continuously. Remove the saucepan from heat when the custard approaches a boil. Continue to stir a minute more to allow steam to release. Dust the top with 1 to 2 tablespoons of the confectioners' sugar to prevent formation of a skin. Allow to cool.

7. To the cooled custard, add the remaining portion of powdered walnuts and the softened butter. With an electric mixer, beat custard on high speed for 5 minutes until it resembles a light cream.

8. Put one of the meringue disks on a serving plate. Using a spoon and spatula or a pastry bag with a fluted tube, cover the meringue with a layer of half the walnut cream. Place the second meringue on top and add a final layer of walnut cream. Sprinkle with confectioners' sugar and garnish with the reserved walnut halves.

Bread Crumb Cake with Walnuts

Gâteau de Pain Perdu aux Noix

SERVES 6 TO 8

> 1 cup walnut pieces
>
> 2 apples
>
> 3 cups milk
>
> ½ cup sugar
>
> 10 slices white sandwich bread
>
> 1 teaspoon pure vanilla extract
>
> 3 eggs
>
> 4 tablespoons caramel syrup or caramel sauce (see Note)
>
> 2 tablespoons chopped pralines or English toffee bits

1. Preheat oven to 375°. Grease and flour a 9-inch springform pan (or 9 inch cake pan). Set aside 8 good walnut halves for garnish. In the bowl of a food processor, coarsely chop the remaining walnuts.

2. Peel and core the apples. Then grate the flesh.

3. While stirring, warm the milk with the sugar. When the sugar is dissolved and the milk is warm, remove from the heat.

4. Cut off and discard the bread crusts. Dice the bread into ¼-inch pieces and place in a large mixing bowl. There should be 3 to 5 cups of bread measured lightly, not packed. Stir the vanilla into the warm sugared milk and pour over the bread. Let soak for 15 minutes.

5. Beat the eggs. With an electric mixer, beat the soaked bread on low speed for half a minute to produce an even mash. Add the beaten eggs, the grated apple, and the chopped walnuts. Pour this mixture into the prepared pan.

6. Bake for 35 minutes. Let cool for 10 minutes. Remove from the pan while still warm. Drizzle liquid caramel or caramel sauce over the top and spread evenly. Sprinkle with chopped praline and garnish with the reserved 8 walnut halves.

Note: Caramel syrup is available bottled in the coffee section of the grocery store, as a coffee additive, or in the dessert section. You can make your own caramel syrup by simmering ⅔ cup sugar and ⅓ cup water for 3 to 4 minutes in a small saucepan, just until light brown.

Honey Cake Roll with Walnuts

Gâteau Roulé au Miel et aux Noix

SERVES 6 TO 8

4 eggs, at room temperature

½ cup sugar

Pinch of salt

⅓ cup sifted flour

4 tablespoons potato starch or cornstarch

Freshly squeezed juice of 1 lemon

⅔ cup honey

1 cup walnut halves, finely chopped

Confectioners' sugar

1. Preheat oven to 375°. Prepare a cake-roll pan, preferably 13 x 9 inches, by lining the bottom with a sheet of greased aluminum foil.

2. Separate the eggs, putting the whites in one large mixing bowl and the yolks in another.

3. Add ⅓ cup of the sugar to the yolks, and beat until the mixture lightens in color.

4. In the second mixing bowl, whip the egg whites with a pinch of salt and the remaining sugar. Sift the flour and starch over the whites and fold gently with a spoon or spatula.

5. Gently fold a third of the egg whites into the yolk mixture. Then, very carefully, fold this mixture into the remaining egg whites with as few strokes as possible to keep the whites airy. Spread the resulting batter in the prepared pan.

6. Bake for **8 minutes**.

7. Meanwhile, blend the lemon juice with the honey and the chopped walnuts.

8. Prepare a cool surface to receive the cake and dampen the surface slightly. At the end of **8** minutes of baking time, remove the cake from the oven, run a knife around the edges to loosen, and lift the cake (still attached to its foil) onto the cool surface, with cake-side up and foil-side down. If the cake looks too dry, spread a damp towel over it for a few moments.

9. Spread the mixture of lemon, honey, and nuts over the hot cake. Gradually peel the foil back and roll the cake up. Place on the serving plate with the seam side down. Just before serving, sprinkle with powdered sugar. Serve the rolled cake sliced, placing a walnut half on each slice to garnish.

Mocha-Walnut Cake

Moka aux Noix

SERVES 6

2 cups walnut halves

1 cup unsalted butter, softened

*2 teaspoons coffee extract or 2 teaspoons powdered instant coffee mixed
with 1 tablespoon of hot water*

3 whole eggs and 2 egg yolks

¾ cup sugar

⅓ cup sifted flour

4 teaspoons Grand Marnier or other orange-flavored brandy

1. Preheat oven to 375°. Grease and flour a 9-inch springform pan or 9-inch cake pan.

2. Reserve 7 of the best walnut halves for garnish. Use the fine grating disk of a food processor to reduce the remaining walnuts to a fine powder. Put ⅓ aside for the walnut mocha cream and put the other ⅔ in a large mixing bowl.

3. Add 9 tablespoons butter and half the coffee extract to the powdered walnuts in the mixing bowl and blend. Add the 3 whole eggs, one by one, beating slowly. Sift ½ cup sugar and ⅓ cup flour into the batter and beat until smooth. Pour this batter into the prepared pan.

4. Bake for 35 minutes, or until a knife or cake tester comes out clean. Allow to cool and remove the cake from the pan.

5. Meanwhile, prepare the walnut mocha cream: Put a double boiler over medium heat, making sure that the bottom of the top pot does not touch the hot water in the lower pot. Melt 7 tablespoons of butter in the top of the double boiler. Add ¼ cup sugar and the 2 egg yolks, beating with a

wire whip or electric mixer. Add the rest of the coffee extract, the Grand Marnier, and the remaining walnut powder. Beat until the mixture is smooth.

6. When the cake has cooled and you have removed it from the pan, cut it in half horizontally. Spread half the walnut mocha cream on one round and spread the rest on the top and sides of the cake. Smooth the icing with a spatula. Garnish with the reserved walnut halves.

7. Refrigerate the cake for several hours and serve it chilled.

Honey-Walnut Cake

Gâteau de Miel aux Noix

SERVES 6 TO 8

3 eggs

1 tablespoon sugar

2½ cups walnut halves

½ cup honey

¼ cup milk

¼ cup oil

2 cups sifted flour

Pinch of salt

1. Preheat oven to 350°. Grease and flour a 9-inch springform pan. (Use a 9-inch cake pan if you do not have a springform pan.)

2. Separate the eggs, putting the whites in a large bowl and reserving the yolks for the batter.

3. Beat the eggs whites and sugar until stiff but not dry.

4. Reserve 8 good walnut halves for garnish. Chop the remaining walnuts in the bowl of a food processor and reserve.

5. In a large mixing bowl, beat the egg yolks with the honey. Add the milk, then the oil, flour, salt, and chopped walnuts. Mix until smooth. With a large spoon gently fold in the egg whites just until blended. Pour the batter into the prepared pan.

6. Bake for 30 to 35 minutes, or until rounded and golden on top. Allow to cool. Remove from pan and garnish with the reserved walnut halves.

Honey-Walnut Spice Cake

Pain d'Epices au Miel et aux Noix

SERVES 6 TO 8

> 4 tablespoons unsalted butter
>
> ½ cup honey
>
> ⅓ cup brown sugar
>
> 1 egg
>
> ½ cup milk
>
> 2 cups sifted flour
>
> ½ teaspoon baking powder
>
> 1 teaspoon baking soda
>
> 1 teaspoon ground cinnamon
>
> 1 cup walnut pieces, coarsely chopped

1. Preheat oven to 350°. Grease the sides of a 9-inch cake pan and line the bottom with greased waxed paper.

2. Melt the butter over low heat. Add the honey and sugar and blend. Pour into a large mixing bowl and allow to cool.

3. To the cooled ingredients in the mixing bowl, add the egg and milk, and blend. Sift the flour, baking powder, baking soda, and cinnamon into the batter and beat for 1 minute. Finally, add the chopped walnuts and mix until smooth. Pour the batter into the prepared pan.

4. Bake for 1 hour. Allow to cool for 10 minutes. Remove the cake from the pan and peel back the waxed paper. Continue cooling on a cake rack.

Pastries, Cookies, Confections, and Breads

LES BISCUITS, LES CONFISERIES ET LES PAINS

Walnut Biscuits (left) and Walnut Meringues (right)

Baklava or Flake Pastry with Nuts

Walnut Biscuits

Pastry Wedges with Walnut-Nougat Filling

Walnut–Chocolate Chip Cookies

Walnut Wafers

Walnut Macaroons

Walnut Meringues

Walnut Masquerades

Chocolate-Covered Walnuts

Walnut Curls

Walnut Bread

Walnut Bread with Prunes and Figs

Baklava or Flake Pastry with Nuts

Baklavas ou Feuilletés aux Fruits Secs

SERVES 6

> 1 cup walnut pieces
>
> 1 cup pistachios, shelled and unsalted
>
> 1 cup pine nuts
>
> 1½ cups sugar
>
> 6 tablespoons honey
>
> 4 tablespoons unsalted butter
>
> 1 pound phyllo dough or puff pastry, in sheets (ready-made frozen or your own recipe)
>
> Freshly squeezed juice of 1 lemon
>
> 1 tablespoon orange-flower water
>
> 1 tablespoon rosewater, or substitute orange-flower water

1. Preheat oven to 375°. Grease a large, deep baking sheet, preferably rectangular or square.

2. In the bowl of a food processor, coarsely chop the walnuts, pistachios, and pine nuts. Remove the chopped nuts from the food processor. In a mixing bowl, stir ¾ cup of the sugar and 3 tablespoons of the honey into the chopped nuts.

3. Over low heat, melt the butter and remove it from the heat.

4. Spread out half the pastry. If you are using frozen pastry, follow package directions about defrosting and unfolding sheets. As quickly as possible, lay 1 sheet at a time in the baking dish and brush each very lightly with melted butter, until the first half of the pastry forms a single layer on the bottom of the pan. You may need to overlap layers or fold over ends in

order to make the sheets fit in a reasonably even layer. It is better to be quick than to be perfect in this step. You should have used about half the melted butter. If you have used more, melt a little more butter for use in laying the next pastry layer.

5. Spread the nut-and-honey mixture over the pastry layer in the baking dish. Using the same method as you did with the first half of the pastry, lay the second half of the pastry over the nut and honey mixture. With a sharp knife, cut the pastry into serving-size rectangles. (To keep the knife cutting smoothly, run it under cold water between slices.)

6. Prepare a syrup by heating together the remaining ¾ cup sugar, 3 table-spoons honey, and lemon juice. Stir over medium heat until the syrup thickens and becomes clear. Remove from the heat and add 1 tablespoon each of rosewater and orange-flower water. Allow to cool, and chill in the refrigerator.

7. Bake the baklava for 45 minutes, or until puffed and golden. Remove from the oven. Quickly drizzle the cold syrup all over the hot baklava. Allow to cool.

8. When the baklava is cool and you are ready to serve, cut the pieces out again and arrange them on a serving platter.

Walnut Biscuits

Biscuits aux Noix

MAKES 36 BISCUITS

½ cup walnut pieces, coarsely chopped

1⅓ cups flour

1 teaspoon baking powder

½ cup sugar

6 tablespoons unsalted butter, softened

2 tablespoons caramel syrup, in liquid form (see Note)

1. Preheat oven to 350°. Line a baking sheet with aluminum foil.

2. Sift the flour, baking powder, and sugar into a mixing bowl. Add the butter and mix well. Add the chopped walnuts and the liquid caramel syrup and mix well. The dough will be thick and firm.

3. Form the dough into balls the size of a walnut. Place them on the lined baking sheet at 2-inch intervals.

4. Bake the biscuits for 15 minutes, or until golden. Cool on a rack.

Note: Caramel syrup is available bottled in the coffee section, as a coffee additive, or in the dessert section. You can make your own caramel syrup by simmering ⅓ cup sugar and 2 tablespoons water for 3 to 4 minutes in a small saucepan, just until light brown. If your caramel syrup is not liquid at the time you need to add it to the batter, warm it until it liquefies.

Walnut-Nougat Pastry

Biscuit Fourré à la Nougatine aux Noix

MAKES 12 PASTRIES

1 pound sweet tart dough (double the recipe for **Pâte Sablée** *on page 133)*

¾ cup sugar

1¼ cups walnut pieces, coarsely chopped

¼ cup milk

4 tablespoons unsalted butter, at room temperature

1 egg

1. Preheat oven to 400°. Grease and flour a tart pan with a removable bottom.

2. Divide the dough into two pieces; a ⅔ and a ⅓ portion. Roll out the larger portion of the dough and place it in the tart pan, pinching or fluting the edge. Prick the dough with a fork in several places, and sprinkle with a teaspoon of the sugar. Roll out the remaining dough into a circle that will later cover the tart pan. Set this circle aside.

3. In a heavy-bottomed saucepan, lightly brown the sugar over medium heat. Add the chopped walnuts and milk and stir well. Add the butter and stir until the mixture is smooth. Remove from the heat.

4. Pour this hot mixture into the prepared crust. Carefully spread over the bottom of the pastry. In a small bowl, beat the egg. Use a pastry brush to brush the edges of the tart with beaten egg. Place the reserved pastry circle over the tart. Trim the edges and pinch or flute them. Prick the top of the tart with a fork and brush the top with the remaining beaten egg.

5. Bake for 35 minutes, or until the pastry becomes light golden. Cool and serve in wedges.

Walnut–Chocolate Chip Cookies

Cookies aux Noix

MAKES 50 COOKIES

1 cup unsalted butter, softened

¼ cup sugar

⅓ cup light brown sugar

2 eggs

3 cups flour

2 teaspoons baking powder

3 cups walnut pieces, coarsely chopped

1 cup semisweet chocolate chips

1. Preheat oven to 375°. Line a baking sheet with aluminum foil.

2. In a mixing bowl, beat the butter until soft. Add the two kinds of sugar and beat until creamy and lightened in color. Beat in the eggs.

3. Stir the flour and baking powder gradually into the cookie dough, stirring only enough to blend. Add the chopped walnuts and chocolate chips and stir gently to mix in.

4. Drop the dough from a teaspoon onto the lined baking sheet, shaping it into a round as you roll it off the teaspoon. Space the cookies well apart, about 12 to a standard baking sheet. Flatten the rounds slightly with the back of a clean spoon.

5. Bake for 10 to 15 minutes. Allow to cool on the baking sheet before serving.

Walnut Wafers

Croquants aux Noix

2 eggs

½ cup sugar

Pinch of salt

2 cups flour

½ cup crème fraîche or cultured sour cream

1 cup walnut pieces, finely chopped

1. Preheat oven to 325°. Grease and flour a baking sheet and set aside.

2. In a mixing bowl, beat the eggs with the sugar and salt until creamy. Gradually sift in the flour, beating to mix. Continue to beat, adding the crème fraîche and then the chopped walnuts. When the ingredients are well mixed, gather the dough into a ball. Cover the ball with a cloth or plastic wrap, and chill in the refrigerator for 2 hours or more before rolling.

3. Roll out the dough to a thickness of ⅓ inch. (Use as little flour as possible to dust the rolling surface and rolling pin. A pastry cloth and rolling pin cover will minimize the use of flour in rolling.) With a cookie cutter, cut the dough into small rounds and place them on the prepared baking sheet.

4. Bake for 30 minutes. Cool before serving.

Walnut Macaroons

MAKES 30 COOKIES

> *2 cups walnut pieces*
>
> *3 egg whites*
>
> *1¼ cups sugar*

1. Preheat oven to 300°. Lightly brush 2 baking sheets with vegetable oil and dust them with flour. In the bowl of a food processor, use the fine grating blade to reduce the walnuts to a fine powder.

2. In a mixing bowl, beat the egg whites until soft peaks form. While beating, gradually add the sugar. Finally, add the walnut powder and beat just until blended.

3. Drop the batter from a teaspoon onto the prepared baking sheets. Bake for about 30 minutes, without allowing the macaroons to brown. Remove macaroons from the baking sheet and cool them on a rack.

Walnut Meringues

Meringues aux Noix

1 cup walnut pieces

¾ cup confectioners' sugar

3 egg whites

1. Preheat oven to 210°. Lightly brush 2 baking sheets with vegetable oil and dust with flour. In the bowl of a food processor, use the fine grating blade to reduce the walnuts to a fine powder.

2. Bring 2 inches of water to a simmer in a large roasting pan into which you will be able to fit the mixing bowl.

3. In a heatproof mixing bowl, stir the confectioners' sugar and egg whites until well mixed. Place the bowl in the simmering water and turn off the heat. Beat the egg whites and sugar with an electric mixer at high speed until thick and foamy. Remove the bowl from the water and continue to beat until the mixture is stiff and cool.

4. Gently fold in the walnut powder.

5. Use a pastry bag with a fluted nozzle to form meringues on the lined baking sheets in the shape you desire—from quarter-size peaked cookies to cup-round circles for serving with fruit or ice cream.

6. Allow to set in the oven for 1 hour. Avoid browning.

Walnut Masquerades

Noix Déguisées

MAKES 25 CANDIES

1 cup blanched almonds, processed to powder consistency

⅔ cup confectioners' sugar

¼ cup cocoa

1 egg white

50 walnut halves

1. In the bowl of a food processor, mix the almond powder, confectioners' sugar, and cocoa. Gradually add the egg white.

2. Refrigerate for 1 hour. Then form the almond paste into ½-inch balls. Put 1 ball in between 2 walnut halves and press gently to make a "sandwich," creating a whole walnut. Continue until all ingredients are used. (These walnut confections can be kept up to 8 days in the refrigerator, if they are kept in a sealed container.)

Chocolate-Covered Walnuts

Noix Enrobées

MAKES 50 CANDIES

4 ounces dark chocolate

4 tablespoons unsalted butter

50 walnut halves

Unsweetened (bitter) cocoa powder

1 candy thermometer

1. Chop the chocolate coarsely and melt it, with the butter, in a double boiler over simmering water. Stir well with a spatula. When the chocolate is smooth, remove it from the heat and let cool slightly.

2. When the chocolate has cooled to about 95°, gently stab a walnut half with a needle so that you can pick the walnut half up and lower the walnut into the chocolate. Then roll the chocolate-covered walnut in the bitter cocoa. Place it on a rack or on waxed paper dusted with cocoa to cool. Repeat with all the walnuts.

Walnut Curls

Tuiles aux Noix

MAKES 20 CANDIES

¾ cup walnut pieces

¾ cup sugar

1 teaspoon pure vanilla extract

½ cup flour

2 eggs

Pinch of salt

4 tablespoons unsalted butter, melted

1. Preheat oven to 425°. Grease and flour a baking sheet. In the bowl of a food processor, very finely chop the walnuts.

2. In a mixing bowl, beat the sugar, vanilla, flour, eggs, and salt. Mix in the melted butter and chopped walnuts. Let stand 1 hour in a cool place.

3. Form each cookie by rolling 1 tablespoon of dough into a ball, placing it on the baking sheet, and pressing it flat with a clean wet fork. Leave about 3 inches between cookies.

4. Bake for 5 minutes, or just until the cookies brown. Quickly remove cookies with a spatula and turn them over a rolling pin or other curved surface (such as a glass or jar) to shape them into curls. Let them cool over the curved surface before removing.

5. Serve with sherbet.

Walnut Bread

Pain aux Noix

1 LARGE ROUND LOAF

1 package active dry yeast

2½ cups warm water

1 tablespoon sugar

1 tablespoon vegetable oil

6 cups all-purpose flour

2 cups walnut pieces, coarsely chopped

1 egg yolk

1 teaspoon salt

1. Dissolve yeast in 1 cup of the warm water. Add sugar, stir, and set aside.

2. Grease the interior of an enamel-bottomed stew pot or other large, round ovenproof dish with a lid.

3. Pour the flour into a large mixing bowl. Add the chopped walnuts, stir, and then, with your spoon, form a hollow in the center of the flour.

4. In a separate bowl, lightly beat together the egg, the soaked yeast, and salt. Gradually stir this mixture into the hollow of the flour. Gradually add the remaining 1½ cups water and work the dough until well blended.

5. Knead the dough for 10 minutes.

6. Form the dough into a round and place in the oiled pot. Turn it once so that the whole surface of the dough is greased. Cover the pot with a damp cloth and allow the dough to rise for 2 to 3 hours in a warm place.

7. Preheat the oven to 375°.

8. When the dough has doubled in volume, place the lid on the pot. Bake for 1 hour.

9. Remove from the oven, and let the pot stand for 10 minutes. Then lift the lid and remove the bread from the pot. Allow the bread to cool.

Walnut Bread with Prunes and Figs

Pain de Fruits Secs

2 ROUND LOAVES

½ *cup raisins*

¾ *cup walnut pieces*

1 *cup pitted prunes*

½ *cup dried figs*

3 *tablespoons kirsch or other cherry brandy*

1 *teaspoon ground cinnamon*

2 *teaspoons zest of orange*

2 *teaspoons zest of lemon*

1 *recipe* Walnut Bread *dough (see page 175) or frozen ready-made dough for 2 loaves white bread*

1 *egg yolk*

1. Prepare dough for walnut bread up through step 5 (or unwrap and thaw the frozen dough in a warm place). Lightly oil or grease 2 baking sheets.

2. Soak the raisins in a bowl of warm water for 15 minutes. Meanwhile, coarsely chop the walnuts and dice both the prunes and the figs into ¼-inch pieces. In a small bowl, sprinkle the kirsch over the diced fruits and walnut pieces.

3. If the dough has begun to rise, punch it down. Work into the dough the diced fruit and chopped nuts, the cinnamon, and orange and lemon zest. Knead for a few minutes. Form the dough into 2 balls, place 1 on each prepared baking sheet and cover it with a damp, well-wrung cloth. Let these balls rest 30 minutes in a warm place. (If you made the dough according to the preceding walnut bread recipe, incorporate the diced fruit and other

additions as indicated for this step and then let the dough rest 2 to 3 hours covered with a damp, well-wrung cloth.)

4. Preheat the oven to 375°.

5. Remove the cloth cover from each ball of dough and brush with beaten egg yolk. Bake for 30 to 40 minutes. Test for doneness by lifting the loaf from the baking sheet and tapping the bottom. It should make a hollow sound. Remove the loaves from the oven.

6. Cool before slicing.

Ice Creams and Frozen Desserts

Les Glaces et Les Desserts Glacés

Coffee-Walnut Ice Cream

Honey-Walnut Ice Cream

Frozen Nougat with Walnuts

Banana-Walnut Sherbet

Coffee-Walnut Ice Cream

Glace au Café et aux Noix

SERVES 6

Any ice-cream mix is best prepared the night before, so as to be well chilled before placing in the ice-cream maker.

2 cups whole milk

6 egg yolks

⅔ cup sugar

2 tablespoons coffee extract, or 2 tablespoons powdered instant coffee mixed with 2 tablespoons hot water

1 tablespoon crème fraîche or heavy cream

¾ cup walnut pieces

¼ cup chocolate-covered coffee beans

1. Bring the milk to a boil over low heat. Set aside.

2. In a mixing bowl, beat the egg yolks and sugar until light and creamy. Add the scalded milk, beating continuously. Return this mixture to the heat and cook 8 minutes without boiling, stirring continuously. Remove from the heat and add the coffee extract. Mix and refrigerate, preferably overnight. Check whether your ice-cream maker requires putting parts of the machine in the freezer overnight. If so, follow manufacturer's directions.

3. Pour the chilled mix into the ice-cream maker and process for 15 minutes. Add the crème fraîche and continue to process.

4. Meanwhile, finely chop the walnuts and the chocolate-covered coffee beans in the bowl of a food processor.

5. When the ice cream begins to thicken and freeze, add the chopped walnuts and coffee beans. Finish the freezing process and place the frozen ice cream in the freezer for at least 1 hour before serving.

6. Scoop into ball shapes and arrange the balls in goblets or glass cups.

Honey-Walnut Ice Cream

Glace au Miel et aux Noix

SERVES 6

Any ice-cream mix is best prepared the night before, so as to be well chilled before placing in the ice-cream maker.

>   *2 cups whole milk*
>
>   *4 egg yolks*
>
>   *⅓ to ½ cup honey, to taste*
>
>   *¾ cup walnut pieces, finely minced*
>
>   *¼ cup caramel syrup in liquid form (see Note)*

1. Bring the milk to a boil over low heat.

2. In a heavy saucepan, beat the egg yolks and honey until creamy and light in color. Gradually add the boiling milk, beating continuously. Cook over low heat 8 minutes, stirring continuously and avoiding boiling. Remove from heat. Chill rapidly. Hold in the refrigerator until completely chilled, preferably overnight. Check whether your ice-cream maker requires putting parts of the machine in the freezer overnight.

3. Pour the chilled mixture into the ice-cream maker and process according to manufacturer's directions until an ice-cream texture has developed.

4. In a small bowl, mix together the minced walnuts and the liquid caramel.

5. When the ice cream has the right texture, add the mixture of walnuts and caramel. Mix well with the ice cream and freeze at least 1 hour.

6. Scoop into ball shapes, and arrange the balls in goblets or glass cups.

Note: Caramel syrup is available bottled in the coffee section of the grocery store as a coffee additive, or in the dessert section. You can make your own caramel syrup by simmering ⅔ cup sugar and ⅓ cup water for 3 to 4 minutes in a small saucepan, just until light brown. If your caramel syrup is not liquid at the time you need to use it, warm it until it liquefies.

Frozen Nougat with Walnuts

Nougat Glacé aux Noix

SERVES 6

2 teaspoons gelatin

¼ cup raisins

1 tablespoon kirsch or cherry brandy

¾ cup sugar

¾ cup walnut pieces, coarsely chopped

1 cup crème fraîche or heavy cream

⅓ cup candied cherries, halved

¼ cup honey

3 egg whites

Pinch of salt

A few drops of freshly squeezed lemon juice

6 walnut halves, for garnish (optional)

1. Soak the gelatin in ¼ cup water.

2. Soak the raisins in the kirsch.

3. In a heavy saucepan, prepare the caramel by heating ¼ cup of the sugar and 2 tablespoons of water. Stir over low heat until the syrup browns. Remove from the heat and add the chopped walnuts. Immediately pour this nougat onto an oiled marble surface or oiled aluminum foil. When the nougat is solid and cool, chop it into small pieces.

4. In a cold bowl, beat ¾ cup of the crème fraîche until airy, like whipped cream. Add the candied cherries, drained raisins, honey, and chopped nougat.

5. Add soaked gelatin and its liquid to remaining ¼ cup of crème fraîche.

6. In a mixing bowl, beat the egg whites and the remaining ½ cup of sugar. Place the bowl in a baking pan filled part way with boiling water. Add the

salt and lemon juice to the whites and beat rapidly until they are thick and snow white. Remove the bowl from the hot water and allow it to cool, continuing to beat the whites for 30 more seconds.

7. Fold the mixture of crème fraîche and gelatin into the whipped crème fraîche and fruits. Carefully fold in the beaten egg whites, stopping just before the mixture is fully blended. Pour into a springform cake pan and place the pan in the freezer at its coldest setting for 24 hours.

8. Unmold the frozen nougat by plunging the cake pan into warm water for 3 seconds, removing it, running around the rim a knife over which you have run warm water, and then opening the spring. Serve it in slices. Garnish each slice with a walnut half.

Banana-Walnut Sherbet

Sorbet de Bananes aux Noix

SERVES 6

1 cup sugar

1 cup water

6 bananas, peeled

Freshly squeezed juice of 2 lemons

¾ cup walnut pieces, coarsely chopped

*2 tablespoons crème de banane liqueur, or 1 teaspoon banana extract
    plus 1 tablespoon Calvados or other brandy*

1. Heat sugar and water together, stirring until the sugar is dissolved, and cook 2 minutes to a syrup. Let cool.

2. Put bananas in a large bowl and mix them with the crème de banane liquor, the cooled syrup, and the lemon juice.

3. Stir in the walnuts.

4. Freeze in an ice-cream maker according to manufacturer's directions.

Jams and Compotes

LES CONFITURES

Compote of Dried Fruits

Fig and Walnut Jam

Walnut Jam

Green-Walnut Jam

Walnut-Grape Jam

Compote of Dried Fruits

Compote de Fruits Secs

SERVES 6

> 1½ cups pitted prunes
>
> 1½ cups dried figs
>
> 1½ cups dried apricots
>
> 1½ cups raisins
>
> 2 cups water
>
> 2 cups walnut halves
>
> ½ cup sugar

1. Soak the prunes, figs, apricots, and raisins in at least 2 cups water (enough to cover the fruit) for 4 hours. Meanwhile, blanch the walnut halves by boiling them in water for 3 minutes, draining them, and then rubbing off the dark skin.

2. Drain the soaked fruits, reserving the water. In a large pot, over low heat, bring to a simmer 2 cups of the soaking water, the soaked fruits, and the sugar. Simmer until fruit is nearly tender. Remove from heat and allow to cool.

3. Serve cool, decorated with blanched walnut halves.

Fig and Walnut Jam

Confiture de Figues et Noix

MAKES 4 CUPS

2 pounds fresh figs

Sugar (see below for amount)

2 cups walnut pieces, coarsely chopped

1. Start the jam the day before serving: Prick each fresh fig with a fork in several places. Plunge the figs into a large pot of boiling water and continue boiling for 15 minutes.

2. Drain the figs and weigh them. Measure out an equal weight of sugar. (Or measure the figs in cups and measure out an equal number of cups of sugar.)

3. Place alternating layers of figs and sugar in a bowl. Cover the bowl and place it on the bottom shelf of the refrigerator overnight.

4. The next day, place the chopped walnuts and the fig-and-sugar mixture into a heavy enamel or stainless-steel pan. Bring this mixture to a simmer, stirring it at regular intervals. Simmer until the syrup thickens (about 15 to 30 minutes).

5. Meanwhile, sterilize your jam jars: Fill each jar with water up to ¾ full. Place the lid loosely (not screwed tightly) on the jar. Place the jars in a baking pan filled with 1 inch of hot water. Simmer the water in the baking pan for 15 to 20 minutes. Jars and lids will then be sterile.

6. When jam is ready, skim any foam from its top. Fill your sterile jam jars immediately and seal them well. Turn the jars upside down and allow them to cool in this position.

Walnut Jam

Confiture de Noix

MAKES 4 CUPS

This traditional Perigordian treat is dreamlike on toast or a croissant for breakfast, delicious and satisfying spread on a plain cookie as a dessert, and sybaritic as a dollop on a piece of pound cake. Use your imagination to enhance all sorts of simple desserts or pastries with this versatile confection.

> *8 cups walnut halves*
>
> *2 cups water*
>
> *2 cups sugar*

1. Blanch the walnut halves by boiling them in water for 3 minutes, draining them, and then rubbing off the dark skin. Finely chop the blanched walnuts in the bowl of a food processor.

2. In a large enamel or stainless-steel pot, prepare a syrup by bringing the water and sugar to a boil over medium heat. Allow to boil slowly over low heat for 10 minutes. Add the chopped walnuts and cook until the jam is dense. Allow to cool just until warm rather than hot.

3. Meanwhile, sterilize your jam jars: Fill each jar with water up to ¾ full. Place the lid loosely (not screwed tightly) on the jar. Place the jars in a baking pan filled with one inch of hot water. Simmer the water in the baking pan for 15 to 20 minutes. Jars and lids will then be sterile.

4. Pour the warm walnut jam into the jars and seal them well. Turn the jars upside down and allow them to cool in this position.

Green-Walnut Jam

Confiture de Noix Vertes

MAKES 6 CUPS

This jam, a homemade tradition in Southwestern France, will be possible only for those of you who have a walnut tree or live in a walnut-growing region where green walnuts can be purchased or begged from friends. Seek out an opportunity to try it.

2 pounds green walnuts in their husks

4 cups sugar

1 cinnamon stick

1. Pick green (unripe) walnuts after the middle of the walnut-growing season. In France, the right time is between the Feast of St. Jean (or Midsummer's Day) on June 21 and Bastille Day on July 14. Check that the nuts are tender and that their husks are not hard.

2. Use gloves to husk the walnuts to avoid staining your fingers. Open the husk and empty out the green walnut at the core. Discard the husk.

3. Wash the green walnuts and then plunge them in a pot of boiling water and cook for 5 minutes. Drain and then soak them in cold water for 2 hours, changing the water twice.

4. Drain the walnuts well. Make a syrup by heating 4 cups sugar and 1 cup of water in a large pot. Cook the syrup until it starts to thicken. Add the walnuts and the cinnamon stick. Cook over low heat for 1 hour, stirring regularly.

5. Meanwhile, sterilize your jam jars: Fill each jar with water up to ¾ full. Place the lid loosely (not screwed tight) on the jar. Place the jars in a baking pan filled with 1 inch of hot water. Simmer the water in the baking pan for 15 to 20 minutes. Jars and lids will then be sterile.

6. Pour the green-walnut jam into the jars and seal them well. Turn the jars upside down and allow them to cool in this position.

Walnut-Grape Jam

Confiture de Raisins et Noix

MAKES 4 CUPS

2 pounds green grapes

Zest of 1 lemon

2 cups walnut pieces, coarsely chopped

1. Remove grapes from the stem. Wash, peel, and seed them. (If you are using seedless grapes, just wash and peel them.)

2. Put the peeled, seeded grapes into an enamel or stainless steel pot and cook them for 15 minutes over medium-low heat, stirring occasionally to avoid sticking or burning. Press the grape syrup through a coarse strainer or use a food mill to strain.

3. Return the strained grape syrup to the pot with the zest of lemon and chopped walnuts. Cook over low heat until the syrup thickens (15 to 30 minutes.) Stir frequently to avoid sticking or burning. Remove from the heat and cool just until warm, not hot.

4. Meanwhile, sterilize your jam jars: Fill each jar with water up to ¾ full. Place the lid loosely (not screwed tight) on the jar. Place the jars in a baking pan filled with 1 inch of hot water. Simmer the water in the baking pan for 15 to 20 minutes. Jars and lids will then be sterile.

5. Pour the warm walnut-grape jam into the jars and seal them well. Turn the jars upside down and allow them to cool in this position.

Liqueurs and Spirits

Les Liqueurs et Les Alcools

Walnut-Husk Liqueur

Walnut-Leaf Wine

Liqueur-Soaked Fruits

Walnut Wine

Walnut Harvest Wine

Walnut-Husk Liqueur

Liqueur de Brou de Noix

MAKES 6 CUPS

This distinctive liqueur will be possible only for those of you who have a walnut tree or live in a walnut-growing region where green walnuts can be purchased or begged from friends. The marination requires 3 months.

20 green (unripe) walnuts in their husks

4 cups eau de vie or brandy

2 cups sugar

1 cup water

1. Pick 20 green (unripe) walnuts after the middle of the walnut-growing season. In France, the right time is between the Feast of St. Jean (or Midsummer's Day) on June 21 and Bastille Day on July 14. Check that the nuts are tender and that their husks are not hard.

2. Chop the green walnuts with their husks on. Fill the jar nearly full with the chopped nut pieces. (Use more than one jar if they do not fit in one.)

3. Warm the eau de vie or brandy until hot, but not yet simmering. Pour the hot brandy over the chopped nuts in the jar. Seal tightly and allow to marinate in a cool place for 2 months. At the end of this time, filter the brandy, rinse and dry the jar, and return the brandy to the jar.

4. Prepare a syrup by heating the sugar and water together in a saucepan. Remove the syrup from the heat as soon as the sugar has dissolved and the liquid has come to a simmer. Allow to cool. Pour the cool syrup into the jar with the filtered brandy and stir. Reseal the jar and let it stand in a cool place for 1 more month.

5. At the end of the month, filter the liqueur again, put it in a bottle, cork or otherwise seal the bottle, and wait a week before consuming (in moderation, of course!). Keep the corked or sealed bottle at room temperature in a cool place.

Walnut-Leaf Wine

Vin de Feuilles de Noyer

MAKES 6 CUPS

This rustic apéritif requires the leaves of a walnut tree, so those of you with a walnut tree in the yard or neighborhood are in luck. Be sure to go out there with your pruning shears at the right time, in midsummer. The marination requires 2 months.

1 pound walnut-tree leaves, cut at the end of June

2 cups eau de vie or brandy

4 cups red wine

1 cup sugar

1. Cut the walnut leaves. If they are dirty or could have come into contact with any sprays, wash and dry them. Hang them to dry in a cool, shady, and airy place for at least a week, or until dry enough to crumble under pressure.

2. Crush the dried leaves with your hands. Place the pieces in a 3-quart jar with a tight lid. Warm the eau de vie until hot but not yet simmering. Pour it over the leaves. Add the red wine and sugar, and stir. Seal the lid and allow to stand for 2 months. Stir from time to time.

3. Filter with a sieve, pour into a bottle, and cork or otherwise seal the bottle. Serve as an aperitif or liqueur in the late afternoon, before dinner, or after dinner.

Liqueur-Soaked Fruits

Fruits et Liqueurs de Vieux Garçon

MAKES 9 CUPS

1¼ cups sugar

1 pot (about 4 cups) black tea

2 cups walnut halves

1¼ cups whole shelled almonds

2 cups pitted prunes

1 cup dried figs

1 cup dried apricots

1⅓ cups raisins

4 cups eau de vie or brandy

1. Dissolve ¼ cup of the sugar in the tea. Put the nuts and dried fruits in a bowl, pour the sweet tea over them just to cover, and soak for 4 hours, stirring occasionally.

2. Near the end of the soaking time sterilize one or more large jars: Fill each jar with water up to ¾ full. Place the lid loosely (not screwed tight) on the jar. Place the jars in a baking pan filled with 1 inch of hot water. Simmer the water in the baking pan for 15 to 20 minutes. Jars and lids will then be sterile.

3. In each jar, layer soaked fruit (and its liquid, if any) alternately with a layer of the remaining 1 cup of sugar until sugar and fruit are all used.

4. Heat the eau de vie or brandy just until hot, not boiling. Pour it over the fruit. Seal the jars tightly, and store in a cool place.

5. Allow the fruit to marinate for 2 months before tasting.

6. Serve one or two of the marinated fruits, with a few tablespoons of the liqueur, to friends who come over in the afternoon or after dinner. Either tea or coffee makes a great accompaniment.

Walnut Wine

Vin de Noix

MAKES 6 CUPS

This distinctively Périgordian aperitif is available all over the southwest of France in commercially bottled form. It can be found in the United States in some specialty wine shops. When walnut wine is nowhere to be found, recipes requiring it can be made with sweet vermouth in which some walnuts have been warmed. However, there is nothing like the real thing. If you can find green walnuts, try the adventure of making your own walnut wine.

25 green (unripe) walnuts in their husks

2 cups eau de vie or brandy

4 cups red wine

¾ cup sugar

1. Pick 25 green (unripe) walnuts after the middle of the walnut-growing season. In France, the right time is between the Feast of St. Jean (or Midsummer's Day) on June 21, and Bastille Day on July 14. Check that the nuts are tender and that their husks are not hard.

2. Chop the green walnuts with their husks on. Place the walnut pieces in the jar.

3. Warm the eau de vie until hot, but not yet simmering. Pour over the walnut pieces in the jar. Add the red wine and sugar, and stir. Seal the jar and let stand for 3 months. Stir from time to time.

4. Filter with a sieve and pour into a bottle. Cork or otherwise seal the bottle.

Walnut Harvest Wine

Vin de Chatons de Noyer

MAKES 6 QUARTS

40 ripe walnuts in their husks (available at harvest time in walnut-growing regions)

4 cups eau de vie or brandy

5 quarts rosé wine or red wine

1 cup rum

4 cups sugar

1 vanilla bean

1. Soak the walnuts in their husks in the eau de vie. Cover and allow to stand for 40 days. Then filter the brandy into a large container, discarding the soaked walnuts and husks.

2. To the filtered brandy, add the rosé, rum, sugar, and vanilla bean. Let stand again for 1 week, stirring occasionally. Pour the liquid through a sieve into bottles. Cork or otherwise seal the bottles.

Bibliography

Abbey, M. et al., "Partial Replacement of Saturated Fatty Acids with Almonds or Walnuts Lowers Total Plasma Cholesterol and Low-Density Lipoprotein Cholesterol," *American Journal of Clinical Nutrition,* 59 (5): 995-9 (May 1994).

Perdue, Lewis. *The French Paradox and Beyond: Live Longer with Wine and the Mediterranean Lifestyle* (Sonoma, California: Renaissance Publishing, 1992).

Sabate, J. et al., "Effects of Walnuts on Serum Lipid Levels and Blood Pressure in Normal Men," *New England Journal of Medicine,* 328 (9): 603-7 (March 4, 1993).

Singh, R.B. et al., "Effect of Antioxidant-rich Foods on Plasma Ascorbic Acid, Cardiac Enzyme, and Lipid Peroxide Levels in Patients Hospitalized with Acute Myorcardial Infarction," *Journal of the American Diatetic Association,* 95 (7): 775-80 (July 1995).

Index